AN APPEALING ACT

An
Appealing
Act

Why People Appeal
in Civil Cases

Scott Barclay

NORTHWESTERN UNIVERSITY PRESS
THE AMERICAN BAR FOUNDATION

Northwestern University Press
Evanston, Illinois 60208-4210

Printed in the United States of America

ISBN 0-8101-1696-0

Library of Congress Cataloging-in-Publication Data

Barclay, Scott.
    An appealing act : why people appeal in civil cases / Scott
Barclay.
        p.   cm.
    Includes bibliographical references.
    ISBN 0-8101-1696-0 (cloth : acid-free paper)
    1. Appellate procedure — United States.   2. Civil
procedure — United States.   3. Judicial process — United
States.   4. Justice, Administration of — United States.
I. Title.
KF9050.B37   1999
347.73'8 — dc21   99-28704
                                                   CIP

This material is based on work supported by the National
Science Foundation under Grant Nos. SBR-9410902 and
SBR-9422669. Any opinions, findings, conclusions, or
recommendations expressed in this material are those of the
authors and do not necessarily reflect those of the National
Science Foundation.

Contents

TABLES

Acknowledgments

This research was funded through three separate grants: a grant from Northwestern University's Office of Sponsored and Research Programs; a grant from the Law and Social Science Division of the National Science Foundation (SES 9216225); and a grant from the Faculty Research Award Program of the University at Albany, State University of New York (FRAP 320 9734Q).

The research relied upon the access to the records and staff of the Court of Appeals of the Circuit Court of Cook County. Chief Justice Harry G. Comerford and Aurelia Pucinski, clerk of the circuit court, granted access to the court's records. However, this research would not have been possible without the assistance of Patricia Formusa, supervisor of the Appeals Section, and her staff—Margaret Arcan, Charlotte Bleich, Irene Ottenfield, and Dottie Spreng.

I would also like to acknowledge the assistance of Chief Justice D. D. Wozniak, (former) chief justice of the Minnesota Court of Appeals, who granted the author open access to the court, its personnel, and its records. In addition, Chief Justice Paul Anderson, chief justice of the Minnesota Court of Appeals, continued such support with equal interest and enthusiasm. The author received invaluable assistance, information, and ideas on the act of appealing from Cindy Lehr, chief staff attorney of the court of appeals. I also am grateful for practical suggestions offered by Mr. Fred Grittner, clerk of the appellate courts, Dr. Wayne Kobbervig, director of research and planning, and Cathy Schmit, assistant to the staff attorneys.

Mr. Joseph Gockowski, civil court administrator of the Ramsey County Courthouse, and his deputy, Ms. Barbara Hanggi, offered invaluable assistance in accessing nonappellants in St. Paul. Carol Buche was an invaluable research assistant in the St. Paul and Minneapolis area.

Chief Justice Armis E. Hawkins granted permission to undertake the research in the Mississippi Supreme Court and Mr. Stephen Kirchmayr, court administrator, provided practical support for the project. Ms. Linda Stone, supreme court clerk, and Ms. Betty Malanchak, deputy supreme court clerk, offered insight into the procedures of the Mississippi court system.

Knowingly or unknowingly, Christopher Anderson, Ibrahim Abu-Lughod, Debra Avant, Tom Birkland, Peter Breiner, Jay Casper, Daniel Chomsky, Tom Church, Ellen Cohn, Shari Diamond, Victoria Farrar-Myers, Sally Friedman, Jerry Goldman, Jane Delahunty-Goodman, Allen Lind, Anne Hildreth, Julia Koschinsky, Ursula Koschinsky, Stephan Machura, Marijke Malsch, Anna-Maria Marshall, Lynn Mather, James Meeker, Laryssa Mykyta, Gregory Nowell, Ronen Shamir, Vicki Smith, Loretta Stalans, Tom Tyler, and Stephen Wasby provided comments upon some or all of the ideas in this book. In addition, the anonymous reviewers of the book manuscript helped bring the present version to reality. Of these people, the anonymous reviewers, Victoria Farrar-Myers, and Julia Koschinsky are the most responsible for ensuring the quality of the current manuscript. Notwithstanding the many hours of their combined effort to the contrary, I take full responsibility for any errors and logical problems that still remain in the text.

Finally, Rachel Drzewicki, Susan Harris, and Susan Betz of Northwestern University Press were incredibly supportive of the book and its ideas. I cannot help but feel that the book found a great home at Northwestern University Press.

I.

The Decision to Appeal

The front page of the *Guardian* of June 6, 1995, reported that two individuals in a civil action had continually appealed a decision of the trial court all the way to the highest court in the British legal system, the House of Lords. What is interesting about this everyday legal event is that the two individuals, who had accumulated "tens of thousands of pounds" in legal costs, were two neighbors fighting over three and a half thousand pounds in damages resulting from a backyard dispute. The decision of the Law Lords to hear this case was berated by the *Guardian,* which subsequently called for improvements in the legal system in order to deal more efficiently with such "low value disputes."

It is no wonder that the *Guardian* called for a more efficient means to deal with such cases because, within the traditional explanation of why individuals appeal in civil cases, the behavior of the litigants in this case is identified as an anomaly. Yet the constituent elements of this British case are typical of the components to be found universally in the appeals of individual civil litigants. First, the majority of litigants who appeal in civil cases appear to be individual litigants rather than governments or corporations (Barclay 1993). Second, these individual litigants often appeal in situations in which the potential benefits are far exceeded by the litigants' own transaction costs (Barclay 1997a). Third, these individual litigants often identify relatively routine disputes as significant enough to require extensive litigation, including resorting to appellate action, in order to achieve a satisfactory resolution (Barclay 1997a). Finally, individual litigants often appeal in cases that are designated by the legal system as of "low value," and consequently, the traditional response of the legal system has been to deter such appeals in favor of encouraging higher economic and/or social value cases (Posner 1985, 1996).

In addition to their role as representatives of individual civil litigants, the two individuals in this British story are familiar to us on another level.

They are the realization of the shouted threat of an aggrieved person to take their grievance all the way to the highest court in the land in order to receive justice: "This is unjust and I will take this all the way to the House of Lords [High Court, Supreme Court, Verfassungsgericht, etc.] if I have to in order to get justice!" They represent that part of us that refuses to give up on an issue, no matter the personal and financial cost, until it has been resolved to our satisfaction.

In this book, I examine the question: Why do individuals appeal in civil cases? This issue is particularly salient at this time. Many prominent judges believe that appellate courts are currently facing the primary brunt of the "litigation explosion" of the last two decades (e.g., Chapper and Hansen 1990; Gizzi 1993, 97). Appellate judges and court administrators are searching for methods to restrict the recent increase in appeals, while maintaining the legitimacy of the judiciary (Posner 1985, 1996). In addition, this same question has increasingly been on the legislative agenda as legislatures seek to stem the rising costs associated with administering the civil court system as well as lower the caseloads faced by the courts at the appellate level. For example, the United States Congress has introduced more than 37 bills (of which only one has become law) in the last decade in an attempt to restrict civil appeals in the area of torts alone.

Despite these various activities, the current legal literature is devoid of basic research on the concept of why individual litigants appeal in civil cases. The absence of research on this issue occurs because legal scholars simply accept the assumption that litigants are interested only in winning (e.g., Posner 1985, 1986; Landes and Posner 1987; Atkins 1990; Atkins 1993; Barclay 1997a). As Posner (1985, 8) subtly summed up the logic of this idea: "everyone prefers winning to losing and winning big to winning small." Within such an approach, the two British neighbors, who represent the typical appeal by individual civil litigants, are an embarrassing aberration of practice from theory—they appeal in a case in which they stand to lose more than they can possibly win—and the *Guardian* appropriately wants them sanctioned for breaking the norms that are thought to underlie the logic of litigation.

Yet, the fact that this assumption—that people litigate purely because they are motivated to win—is unable to explain the actions of the typical individual civil litigant highlights the problem in simply accepting the current assumption as a valid explanation of why individuals appeal, and it raises the need for a new theory. In contrast to the current assumption, I argue that individuals are less interested in winning their cases than we have been traditionally led to believe. Instead, I posit that the litigants are motivated primarily by the desire to be treated fairly. This new motivation is counter to the current focus on rational actors and the outcome of court decisions. It is only by such a complete reorientation of our current perspective on what motivates individuals that we will be able to explain a variety of the activities displayed by individuals in relation to the courts, including the decision to appeal.

Using these two different motivations—the desire to win versus the desire to be treated fairly—as a basis, I demonstrate that there are two possible approaches to the decision to appeal: an outcome-based approach and a process-based approach. The outcome-based approach views individuals as motivated by the desire to win. It focuses on the litigants' level of satisfaction with the decision of the trial court as well as the litigants' expected level of satisfaction with the possible results of any ensuing appellate action as the means for understanding the decision to appeal. While the traditional explanations of why individuals appeal have not appeared under this nomenclature, the apparently disparate models that currently purport to explain why individuals appeal actually share this common approach. As such, the outcome-based approach has been the dominant approach adopted, to date, by legal scholars and court administrators. I consider the premises of this approach in relation to the behavior and ideas articulated by real litigants faced with the decision whether to appeal or not.

In contrast to the outcome-based approach, I emphasize the value in adopting a process-based approach, which views individuals as motivated by the desire to be treated fairly. Using Dahl's and Habermas's theories of the political meaning of procedures as well as the findings of the recent procedural justice literature, I develop the outlines of this alternative approach. Such an approach focuses on the litigants' level of satisfaction, based on their perceptions of the procedures used to reach a decision in the trial court action, as well as the litigants' expected level of satisfaction with the procedures to be used by the appellate court, as the means for understanding the decision to appeal. I argue that, if they used models based on a process-based approach, legal scholars would be able to offer a better explanation of the decision to appeal, as well as to develop new insights into court-related violence, individual compliance, and judicial legitimacy.

These two approaches—the outcome-based approach and the process-based approach—are antithetical. Simultaneously, they must be considered as equal counterparts in regard to their ability to offer a theoretical framework through which to understand individual behavior. As I will demonstrate later in this chapter, the approach adopted by litigants in making decisions in their interactions with legal institutions is highly related to the litigants' perceptions of the chance for bias in the court's activities. To date, scholars have focused on the outcome-based approach. The current study is designed to demonstrate the potential offered by its counterpart, the process-based approach. Yet, notwithstanding the fact that the current research indicates that the process-based approach is better able to explain the decision to appeal by individual civil litigants, both approaches need to be treated as theoretically equally valid means for understanding individual behavior, and legal scholars need to recognize the duality of approaches that exist for understanding the behavior of litigants.

The book has three goals. First, I recognize the disparate current models of why people appeal as sharing a common approach. Second, I develop an alternative approach and demonstrate the potential offered by it in terms of explaining the decision to appeal as well as other individual behavior in the courts. Third, I identify the two approaches as antithetical, such that we must acknowledge that each offers a potentially equal framework for understanding individual behavior. I also consider the implications of such a finding for the way that legal scholars conduct research on individuals in the courts, including how they approach the decision to appeal. Although I focus on individual behavior within the courts, specifically using the example of the decision whether to appeal in civil cases, the two current approaches appear to encapsulate the two possible frameworks that could be used by scholars to understand individual behavior in a variety of noncourt settings. As such, the real value of this book lies in reframing the current debate in a way that recognizes these two approaches when attempting to explain the behavior of individuals in general in their interaction with political or legal institutions.

To explore these two approaches, I use data drawn from the first systematic interviews in the United States of individual civil litigants on the question of why people appeal: 125 qualitative interviews with individual civil litigants in four court sites—three appellate courts and a trial court. This data was designed to allow the litigants to discuss their court experiences in their own words, and this book is the first work to address the decision to appeal using the voices of those actually involved in the decision.

Based on the evidence of these stories, I propose that we cannot simply accept the assumption that most people appeal purely because of the money involved. Instead, I argue that people are more interested in having someone in authority consider their legal claims fairly than they are in what they may win in the end. In fact, I propose that given a choice between winning and the ability to be treated with respect by the courts, most losing litigants choose the latter. While, at first glance, this appears contrary to our intuition of what motivates litigants, this concept is consistent with what we have long acknowledged as an important aspect of litigation: the desire in each litigant to receive justice through the satisfactory resolution of their dispute. It returns us to our earlier example of the litigant who takes his or her case all the way to the highest court in the pursuit of justice. In highlighting this aspect, I offer an alternative method of viewing not only the decision to appeal but also the litigants themselves.

Because my goal is to expand our consideration of what motivates individual behavior, my focus is on the decision whether to appeal as exercised by individual civil litigants. Notwithstanding the fact that companies and government agencies are also involved in litigation at the appellate level, the present discussion does not include consideration of the different role that these entities play in the appellate arena in comparison to individual litigants (e.g., Galanter 1974; Eisenstein 1978). Such a focus need not detract from the value of the book since individual civil litigants constitute a substantial portion of the appellant population; for example, in a sample of civil appeals filed in the Minnesota Court of Appeals in May 1992, individual civil litigants were appellants in 62 percent of the filed civil cases, and individual litigants were parties in 72 percent of the civil appellate actions for the month.

Table 1 outlines the relationship between the two approaches as they will be portrayed throughout the book. The ideas outlined in this table will be elaborated in the remainder of this chapter.

The Social and Political Consequences of the Decision to Appeal

On a political level, the decision to appeal is important because, through the initiation of an appeal, a litigant explicitly or implicitly challenges a current policy of the state. The trial court decision determines the nature of

TABLE 1
TWO APPROACHES TO APPEALING

Outcome-Based Approach	Process-Based Approach
Assumed primary motivation of individuals	**Assumed primary motivation of individuals**
The desire to win	The desire to be treated fairly in resolving their disputes
Current models	**Current models**
Cost/benefit model	None
Political model	
Individual resources model	
Characteristics	**Characteristics**
Focuses on the result of the court case in terms of winning or losing	Focuses on the process used to reach an outcome in each case in terms of its fairness or unfairness
Begins from the premise that every losing litigant is a potential initiator of an appeal	Rejects the notion that every losing litigant is a potential initiator of an appeal
Subsumes process by treating the process as neutral in determining outcome	Subsumes outcome by treating it as a neutral product of the process
Measure of satisfaction	**Measure of satisfaction**
Perception and expectation of outcome	Perception and expectation of process
Metric for assessing the courts' actions	**Metric for assessing the courts' actions**
Distributive justice	Procedural justice
Implications	**Implications**
Court is not an entity in considering court-related violence, compliance, and legitimacy	Court is an entity in considering court-related violence, compliance, and legitimacy
Process should not matter as long as it is not suspected to be biased	Outcome should not matter as long as it is not suspected to be biased

government policy as it applies to the litigant and all other potential litigants (Mnookin and Kornhauser 1979). In this context, the trial court decision represents the articulation of state policy in relation to the litigant. Such policy is state-created; that is, laws are the creation of legislatures, the executive branch, and the courts. It has state sanction; that is, the laws can be enforced by agents of the state, such as the police or military. Therefore, it represents state policy. Extrapolating from the ideas of Zemans (1983) and Lawrence (1991a, 1991b), we can identify that even if the litigant thinks that the trial court has simply made an error in articulating the existing law, by appealing, the litigant is still challenging the articulated policy of the state. By refusing to accept the initial decision of the government (in this case represented by the opinion of the trial court), the appellant establishes an interactive process between herself and the government (in this case represented by the judiciary), in which she directly questions the decision of a government agency (in this case represented by the trial court). Whether aware of it or not, she seeks to alter—by appealing for a different decision—the articulated policy of the government, in the form of the trial court decision. In this sense, the appellant is most like her lobbyist counterparts in the halls of the legislature or her protesting counterparts in the streets. She is attempting policy change through an ongoing "dialogue" with a policy-making institution (Lawrence 1991a).

Because appealing is one of the very few avenues that offers individuals direct access to the policy-making apparatus of the state, there appears to be general agreement that the avenue of appeal is an important characteristic in maintaining the legitimacy of a regime (Shapiro 1980; Dalton 1985; Tyler and Rasinski 1991; Baum 1994). Therefore, even though most appeals are unlikely to prevail (Songer and Sheehan 1992), the ability of individuals to appeal decisions of the state helps to ensure that the political system has, at least in appearance, some method of incorporating the political demands of the citizenry. Consequently, the ability to appeal propagates the idea that citizens need not seek alternative methods, including rebellion or revolution, in order to have their political demands incorporated into the state's policy-making process (Shapiro 1980).

Because of this important role in legitimating the political system, almost every government within every type of regime has some institutionalized avenue of appeal and "the right to appeal at least once without prior court approval is nearly universal" (Dalton 1985, 62). Unlike many other individual decisions involving the state, such as voting (e.g., Scarbrough

1984), the decision to appeal can be identified as one of the select individual decisions that exists in a relatively similar format in a variety of regimes and historical junctures. Consequently, understanding this choice can offer important insights into human political behavior in a wide range of political and social systems.

Notwithstanding the fact that the decision to appeal can be interpreted as a political act, on the face of it, it might appear that this decision lacks the apparent claim to social controversy or political relevance associated with many similar such individual decisions. For example, in the case of an individual deciding whether to enlist in order to fight in a war, the social controversy attached to the final outcome of each individual's decision lends pertinence to each individual's choice irrespective of other relevant factors. Furthermore, the choice of whether to appeal lacks even the apparent political relevance associated with the decision to vote, because the choice about appealing is restricted to a very limited segment of the society (Yankelovich, Skelly, and White 1977; Shapiro 1980; Galanter 1983, 21; Dalton 1985; Songer and Sheehan 1992; Atkins 1993).

Yet such simple choices are the mainstays of social science, because it is assumed that from understanding such choices we can gain insight into what motivates people to act in a political and social context. Such understanding is identified as important, not only on the abstract level of self-realization, but because of the importance of the consequences that accrue from the cumulative choices made by individuals in regard to the political and social context. If each person chose not to fight in a war, there would be no war. If each person chose not to vote, there would be no elections. Consequently, if we think wars and elections are important parts of the political and social context, we must understand why individuals choose to participate in these activities. A similar logic is apparent in regard to the choice about appealing. Just as in the case of voting, the decision whether to appeal occurs in a context in which the accumulation of the individual decisions has important consequences in regard to the subsequent ability of the judiciary to make and shape social policy. The decision of some individual litigants to appeal shapes the pool from which the appellate courts subsequently select cases; just as the decisions of voters cumulate to form a collective choice on issues or institutional representatives, so do individual decisions to appeal cumulate to create a form of political mobilization to which the appellate courts respond (Zemans 1983; Lawrence 1991b). Individual decisions to appeal cumulate to shape the case pool of courts in two practical ways: the size of the case pool and the substantive nature of the cases within the case pool.

While each individual litigant chooses whether to appeal, the cumulative effect of these individual decisions determines how many cases each appellate court must resolve in any period. According to the legal literature, judges feel that the number of the appellate court filings has increased disproportionately in the last three decades in regard to the relative size of the appellate arena (Posner 1985, 1996; cf. Galanter 1993). In response to this perceived increase in caseload, appellate judges and court administrators are searching currently for methods to restrict the number of civil appeals while simultaneously maintaining the legitimacy of the judiciary (Posner 1985; *Guardian,* November 14, 1995, 10). In such a context, it is very important to understand the motivation of litigants for appealing in order that the judicial system, if it so chooses, can respond to this perception of an increase in appellate filings in a manner that does not detract from the legitimacy and purpose of the judiciary.

Each individual decision to appeal also determines which types of cases the courts must resolve. As the earlier *Guardian* example demonstrates, the popular media perceives that the type of cases being considered by appellate courts has changed. There has been a growing criticism of appellate courts based on the notion that they are increasingly resolving "political issues" to the detriment of traditional legal decision making. While not new (cf. Hamilton 1788; Cox 1976), this argument has been at the heart of recent attempts to restrict the jurisdiction of the judiciary in the appellate arena in the United States, as evidenced by the myriad of proposals for law reform introduced in the U. S. Congress since 1990.[1] In addition, this argument has been used by the popular media as part of their explanation of the apparently increasingly political nature of several formerly "apolitical" national appellate courts; for example, the recent decisions on aboriginal sovereignty (*Mabo v. Queensland [No. 1]* 166 C.L.R. 186; *The Wik Peoples v. The State of Queensland* Matter No. B8 of 1996) of the High Court of the Commonwealth of Australia and the recent decisions on abortion by the Constitutional Court (Bundesverfassungsgericht) of the Federal Republic of Germany have been taken as evidence of the increasingly political nature of these courts. While such an argument usually overlooks a long history of political decisions by such courts, the argument is important in the current context because it is based in part on the notion that there has been an increase in the political nature of the many individual civil cases that are brought to the appellate courts for resolution. If it is true that more "political" cases are being appealed, it is important to understand why individual losing litigants are choosing to take such cases to the courts.

The decision to appeal is important for one final reason that extends beyond the aggregate effect on the political and social system. For the people involved, the decision whether to appeal is often as traumatic as the decisions we associate customarily with more socially controversial issues. Most people do not invoke the courts easily (Merry 1979), and in the case of those who lose in the trial court, these individuals are often faced with an unsatisfactory resolution of a painful series of events associated with the original injury or claim. The decision whether to appeal is not simply a decision whether to continue in the courts but it is also a decision whether to accept any form of resolution in regard to the important life decisions that lie at the core of most civil cases. Concealed within each relatively routine civil case are important life issues in regard to the future of the individual and how the individual chooses to resolve these issues: decisions about ending marriages (marriage dissolutions), resolving oneself to the new physical or emotional conditions imposed by unforeseen circumstances (torts, unemployment compensation), defining one's relationship with others with whom she or he interacts (contract, landlord/tenant, civil rights, discrimination, paternity), and dealing with death (probate). The decision to forgo the resolution of these issues by appealing the trial court's decision means that these individuals also forgo their ability to close that section of their life that relates to the original issue.

The Difference between the Two Approaches

Despite the variety of actions of individuals, we assume that, on the meta-level, people are motivated into action by only a few core desires, such as the desire for happiness, wealth, sex, power, freedom, dignity, equality, or fairness. In regard to the decision to appeal, I will argue that the two approaches posit two differing motivations—the desire to win and the desire to be treated fairly—that stimulate the litigant into action. These two motivations directly relate to whether the litigant will subsequently focus on the outcome or the process in regard to deciding whether to appeal.

Outcome-Based Approach

The outcome-based approach considers litigants as motivated by the desire to win. From this perspective, litigants are interested primarily in the question of outcome—winning or losing—and they can meet their desired goal only by winning. The desire of the litigants to pursue their claims until they win is unquestioned since "everyone prefers winning to losing and winning big to winning small" (Posner 1985, 8). Thus, once a logical reason for the original litigation is posited, it is assumed that the litigants will continue to pursue that goal until they achieve it by winning. Conversely, if the litigants have no opportunity to win, it is assumed that their motivation is eliminated.

This approach begins from a premise that each litigant who loses in the trial court is a potential initiator of an appeal; that is, that people would prefer to prevail rather than to lose and that people accept a loss only because it becomes too difficult to prevail. Since one party always loses and that party would not only prefer to win but *must* win in order to achieve their goal, one party should always want to appeal.[2] Such an approach is premised on the notion that the litigants' desire for their goal will not decrease as long as it is possible to achieve it; that is, as long as they have a possibility of winning. It is the fact of having lost that makes every such litigant a potential initiator of an appeal. Since litigants who lose in the trial court should want to appeal, the outcome-based approach assumes that if there were no transaction costs or legal barriers to appealing, every losing litigant would automatically initiate an appeal. The desire to appeal is removed only when the litigants either (a) fulfill their goals by winning or (b) are precluded from fulfilling their goals by some insurmountable barrier that effectively convinces them that they cannot achieve their goals through continued court action.

In this book, three different models—the *cost/benefit* model, the *individual resources* model, and the *political* model—are used to represent the outcome-based approach, and each is discussed in more depth in the next chapter. While each model begins from the premise that litigants wish to win, each model posits a different goal that the litigants desire to achieve by winning:

- within the *cost/benefit* model, the litigants' goal is to maximize financial gain or minimize financial loss;
- within the *individual resources* model, the litigants' goal is to achieve positive policy precedent;

- within the *political* model, the "ordinary" litigants' goal is to maximize financial gain while the "political" litigants' goal is to advance political goals.

The outcome-based approach assumes pursuing an appeal is rational unless barriers preclude the litigant from appealing. The barriers that would preclude appealing must, by the definition of the approach, be related directly to the litigants' goals. For example, if I appeal in order to maximize my financial gain, the court could eliminate my motivation to appeal by removing the possibility of achieving any financial gain; for example, by restricting the ability to receive any money even if I were to win, such as has been proposed in recent legislative attempts at tort reform. Similarly, the outcome-based approach proposes that the court could eliminate the possibility of appealing by removing the ability to win; for example, the legislature could pass laws that predetermine the outcome of certain classes of cases, such as occurs when the legislature specifically counters existing court decisions with contrary legislation.

Process-Based Approach

The process-based approach considers each litigant as motivated by the desire to be treated fairly. From this perspective, litigants are interested primarily in the question of the process used by the courts in the resolution of their dispute — the fairness or unfairness of the process — and their desired goal is to be heard fairly by someone in authority in regard to the issue that the litigants think is at the heart of their dispute. The litigants enter the courts in the first place in order to resolve their disputes, and they will continue to pursue their claims, either in the courts or by using alternative methods, until such time as they achieve a satisfactory resolution of that original dispute.

Unlike the outcome-based approach, which assumes that litigants can meet their desired goal only by winning, the process-based approach rejects the notion that the litigants need to win in order to achieve their goals. Since the desired goal is simply to have someone in authority consider the litigants' ideas in order to resolve the dispute fairly, it is not essential that the litigants prevail to achieve this goal. If the litigants perceive that their ideas about the dispute have been heard fairly by someone in authority such that their ideas are given due consideration in reaching an outcome, the litigants have achieved their goal even if the subsequent outcome is negative. In this context, winning could also be approached from a more process-based perspective; winning

might be taken as evidence that your ideas have been fairly heard by the decision maker, such that the decision maker is swayed to your position in regard
to the issues at the heart of the dispute. From our own experiences, we know
that there are many times when we accept negative outcomes merely because
we have had the chance to state our ideas as part of the process of reaching the
subsequent outcome—general elections and decision making in faculty meet-
ings might be two immediate examples for academics. In a similar vein, litigants who lose in the trial court can no longer be identified as potential
initiators of an appeal, because those litigants who are satisfied with the process
will not appeal, independent of the subsequent outcome.

Within the process-based approach, the litigants are interested in having their dispute resolved to their satisfaction and they will continue to
want to pursue this action until it is resolved. Even if the litigants are precluded subsequently from appealing, they are still motivated to have their
original dispute resolved, because the end of the dispute occurs only when
they are satisfied with the resolution offered. Therefore, the litigants are
motivated to appeal until either the dispute is resolved to their satisfaction
or the courts demonstrate that the litigants cannot achieve their goal within
the courts. There is one primary manner in which the courts could demonstrate that the litigants cannot achieve their goal within the courts; that
is, to convince the litigants that they will not be heard in a fair manner in
the trial court and that they will also not be heard in a fair manner in the
appellate court. In such a context, the litigants are unlikely to continue to
use the courts to resolve their disputes. However, it should be noted that,
even if the litigants are convinced that they will not be heard in a fair manner in the courts, as long as they do not believe that their dispute has been
satisfactorily resolved, they will seek alternative methods of resolving that
dispute to their satisfaction, such as post-trial settlements as well as other
less socially desirable methods. Similarly, if the courts legally or financially
restrict the litigants' ability to appeal, this should not decrease the litigants'
desire to resolve their disputes and they would seek alternative methods to
achieve such a resolution. From this perspective, the courts can eliminate the
desire to appeal by either treating litigants fairly in the trial court or conversely, by convincing the litigants that they will not be treated fairly if they
enter the appellate court.

Since a process-based approach has been largely absent from legal scholars' prior considerations of the decision to appeal, I develop the parameters
of a process-based approach. In later chapters, I demonstrate that such an

approach is more consistent with the litigants' behavior and their ideas about the decision to appeal.

The Notion of Justice in Each Approach

While each approach considers that the actions associated with appealing are measured according to a notion of justice, the two approaches use divergent concepts of justice as the metric by which to measure the actions of the courts. Both of the approaches propose that people want to receive justice from the courts; but the two approaches differ in their definitions of justice. These divergent concepts of justice follow directly from the differing motivations offered by the two approaches. If individuals are motivated by the desire to win, the metric used to measure whether the outcome is consistent with that desire must focus on a concept of justice that relates to consequences or the outcome — distributive justice is such a concept. On the other hand, if we posit that individuals are motivated by the desire to be treated fairly, the metric used to measure whether the process is consistent with that idea must focus on a concept of justice that relates to the procedures used to arrive at an outcome — procedural justice is such a concept.

In this context, justice is more than an abstract social value. Instead, in the hands of the litigants, it provides the criteria that are used to determine whether the day-to-day activities of the court are consistent with social norms. For example, because of the criteria that generally constitute the notion of parliamentary democracy, we can state clearly that the murder of representatives of opposing factions is not consistent with this notion and such an action would be defined as undemocratic. We can make such a judgment because parliamentary democracy as a concept incorporates the criteria through which we can assess the actions of those people or institutions who are said to embody this concept. Similarly, justice incorporates the criteria that can be used as a means of assessing the activities of the courts in determining whether we would define them as just or unjust. In this sense, justice is not simply a concept to which one may have ideological allegiance, justice is also a method through which one assesses the institutions that are associated with such a concept. In simple terms, litigants assess the courts based on the degree of justice they find in their court experience.

The question remains as to the criteria by which one defines an act as just or unjust. Borrowing from the tradition associated with Bentham

([1789] 1948; see also Hart 1941; Rawls 1971), justice can be split into two separate categories—one category associated with consequences and the other category associated with procedures. This dichotomy has been defined in terms of the distinction between distributive justice and procedural justice. Distributive justice is "concerned with identifying the principles by which anything of value (money, goods, services, privileges, and so forth) can be fairly and equitably allocated among persons and groups" (Thibaut and Walker 1975, 3), whereas procedural justice is concerned with the evaluation of the fairness of the process associated with the allocation of such goods (see also Lane 1988). Using this dichotomy as a basis for distinguishing the two approaches, we can identify that the outcome-based approach uses distributive justice as its yardstick and the process-based approach uses procedural justice as its yardstick. Consequently, while each approach recognizes the importance of a notion of justice in regard to measuring the success of the judiciary in relation to appeals, these two approaches have used very different metrics in measuring whether any individual appeal can be defined as just.

The Relationship between the Two Approaches to Appealing

The two possible approaches to the decision to appeal are antithetical. Therefore, while it is feasible to conceive of a third possible approach, which combines the process and the outcome, such an approach is not possible practically because the two approaches each reduce the focus of the other to an assumption. To explain, the outcome-based approach assumes that the process is a neutral element in determining outcomes, whereas the process-based approach assumes that the outcome is a neutral product of the chosen process. For example, while the process is clearly an important component in determining the outcome, the outcome-based approach treats this component as neutral in the approach, and consequently, the process is not the primary focus. To use the analogy of a coin flip: who flips the coin and how she or he flips it (by hand, by board, by computer) is identified as of little consequence in determining the final outcome. The outcome is seen as shaped by other factors that can be defined objectively; in the case of appeals, by legal precedent or the strength of the evidence. The outcome becomes the only relevant consideration; all else is superfluous unless it can have an impact on determining the outcome in some manner, and the process is not identified as such an element that normally has an impact on the outcome.[3] Similarly, the process-based approach treats the outcome as a neutral product of the process used to arrive at that outcome. To return to the analogy of the coin flip: the process-based approach argues that who flips the coin and how are very important determinants in shaping the range of possible outcomes.

Each approach can impose the assumption of neutrality only as long as there is no indication of bias. For example, in the outcome-based approach, process is treated as neutral only as long as the process is identified as not biased in such an obvious way that the outcome is predetermined. If such a bias is suspected, the outcome-based approach quickly transforms into the process-based approach. To return to the analogy of the coin flip: the flipping of the coin can be treated as a neutral process only as long as no one suspects that the coin is purposely weighted or two-headed. Where the coin is believed to be purposely weighted or two-headed, this presumed bias in the process transforms our analysis into one that relies on a process-based approach. Similarly, the process-based approach can treat the outcome as neutral only as long as the process determines the range. The coin-flip may be fair, but if a biased judge "calls" the outcome to suit his or her wishes, then the outcome is not a neutral product of the process, and the analysis becomes one that relies on an outcome-based approach.

To date, legal scholars have ignored the relationship between the process and the outcome, and they have focused on the outcome-based approach with the assumption that the process can be treated as neutral in determining outcomes. In challenging this approach, it would be possible to simply replicate the traditional framework, such that I focused on the process-based approach with the assumption that the outcome can be treated as a neutral product of the process. To a large extent that is the strategy that I shall adopt throughout most of the book, and I will demonstrate that a process-based approach is more consistent with the behavior and ideas of litigants involved in the decision whether to appeal. However, while the process and the outcome are treated traditionally as largely independent for academic consideration (e.g., Lind and Tyler 1988; Tyler 1990), I will argue that the relationship between these two aspects is essential to understanding the litigants' focus in the decision to appeal. In the current context, it may well be the possibility of bias by the courts that causes the litigants to use the process-based approach in their decision whether to appeal.

Common Aspects of the Two Approaches

The two approaches can be compared and contrasted in a systematic manner because they are actually based on a series of shared premises. While recognizing the aggregate effects that accrue from the cumulation of each individual's decision to appeal, the individual litigant remains the unit of analysis in each approach.

Each approach assumes that litigants will continue to pursue their court actions until they are satisfied. In order to consider the litigants' level of satisfaction, each approach focuses on the litigants' perceptions and their expectations in regard to either the outcome or the process, respectively. Each approach uses the litigants' perceptions in regard to the trial court and their expectations in regard to the appellate court as a basis for understanding their subsequent decisions to appeal. The outcome-based approach focuses on the litigants' perceived loss in the trial court and their expected chance of winning in the appellate court as a basis for understanding their subsequent decision to appeal, whereas the process-based approach focuses on the litigants' perceived unfair treatment in the trial court and their expected chance of being treated fairly in the appellate court.

Finally, each approach offers a universal explanation for the decision to appeal. In the current case, each approach assumes that litigants in a variety of cultures and nations are compelled by common motivations and goals that transcend cultural and national differences.

In the past, these two approaches have on occasion been incorrectly distinguished in terms of objective and subjective assessments. The outcome-based approach has been associated with the notion of an objective result—win or lose. This approach is supposedly in contrast to the litigants' subjective assessments of procedure associated with the process-based approach. However, Kritzer (1984, 1991; Kritzer et al. 1985) has argued that the definition of winning and losing is not a simple assessment observable to outside parties but instead requires understanding of the litigants' original expectations. This latter definition challenges the simple differentiation of these two approaches in terms of identifying them as objective and subjective approaches, respectively. Moreover, it supports the notion that each of these approaches relies on the individuals' perceptions and expectations in determining both outcome and process.

The Practical and Theoretical Implications of Using the Two Different Approaches

At first glance, it might not appear important which of these two approaches legal scholars use in understanding the decision to appeal. In fact, it might appear irrelevant whether individual civil litigants focus on the process or the outcome in their decision to appeal. However, the difference between the process-based approach and the outcome-based approach has important practical and theoretical implications, which can be highlighted by returning to the example from the British legal system that introduced this chapter.

In the British example, the *Guardian* defined the litigation as unworthy of court-based resolution at the appellate level. Yet individual litigants often appeal in cases that are designated by the legal system as of "low value." The traditional response of the legal system has been to deter such appeals in favor of encouraging higher economic and/or social value cases (e.g., Posner 1996). Seeking to deter "low-value" civil cases by individual litigants is consistent with the recent calls by court administrators (see Galanter 1983), judges (see Posner 1985; Dalton 1985; Chapper and Hansen 1990; Gizzi 1993), the media (e.g., the *Guardian*), and legislatures (e.g., the Common Sense Product Liability and Legal Reform Act of 1995 proposed by the 104th U.S. Congress) to restrict the ability of individuals to initiate civil appeals.

Three methods of restricting an increase in appeals have been proposed in recent discussions of the issue (Posner 1985; Dalton 1985). The first method is to restrict the ability of losing litigants to initiate an appeal in regard to certain civil cases, such as tort cases. The second method is to restrict the possibility of losing litigants' "winning big" from such cases by capping the accepted damages awarded by the courts. The final method has been to predetermine the outcome of many such appeals by selective legislation in the specific area, such that there can be no confusion as to which party would prevail in the case of an appeal by the individual litigant. Let us consider the practical implications of each of these three methods in regard to the two approaches.

From a process-based approach, an increase in appeals reflects an increasing perception that the trial court was not fair in their treatment of the claims of litigants but that the appellate court is more likely to be fair in resolving the same disputes. Since the litigants appeal only because they continue to believe that they will be fairly heard in the courts, even if the trial court did not appear fairly to consider their case, an increase in appeals can be identified as an increase in the desire to be heard fairly in the courts notwithstanding the original trial experience. An increase in appeals would signal that a growing number of litigants believed that they were not heard fairly in the trial court. The decision to appeal occurs because they expect that the appellate court will hear their claim in a fair manner in reaching an outcome. In such a context, simply acting to restrict appeals would have adverse effects on the long-term legitimacy of the judiciary. The restriction of appeals would be identified as removing the potential to be heard fairly in the appellate courts from those litigants who felt that they were mistreated in the trial court. Similarly, restricting the ability of the court to fairly compensate litigants for the damages suffered in the original disputes is simply restricting the ability of the court to consider fairly the whole range of possible methods of resolving the dispute. The same holds true if the court's outcome is predetermined by the legislature. In such cases, the eventual outcome is determined by a biased process or the outcome is separated from the process in a manner that makes the process irrelevant. In each case, there exists no reason for the litigants to consider that they have any chance of being heard fairly by the courts. They will conclude that their ideas about the issues at the heart of their dispute will not be considered by the decision maker as part of reaching an outcome. The outcome has been predefined and the courts would be identified as unfair. In response, losing litigants would turn to alternative means in order to resolve their original dispute. In addition, losing litigants, who are frustrated by the lack of fairness that they associate with the trial court, are less likely to obey the edicts of such a court and these same litigants are more likely to turn their ire on the court systems to protest their unfair treatment. The overall impact of acting to restrict appeals in these three manners would be to decrease the legitimacy of the courts and lower the compliance rate of individuals while simultaneously increasing the potential for court-related violence and the use of alternative, and potentially less socially desirable, methods of resolving disputes.

Yet this same scenario, when viewed from the perspective of an outcome-based approach, would lead to very different consequences. From an outcome-based approach, an increase in appeals may reflect an increased potential for winning in the appellate court, which could be resolved by simply restricting the ability to appeal, the ability to "win big" in the courts, or the likely outcome if one appealed. Simply restricting the access of losing litigants to the appellate arena would have no long-term deleterious effects on the legitimacy of the court. The litigants would no longer be motivated to pursue their appeals because their motivation is eliminated by restricting their ability to win. Instead, they are forced to accept the trial court's decision. From an outcome-based approach, the act of restricting the ability to appeal is unlikely to lead to any subsequent increase in court-related violence or noncompliance, nor is it likely to have an impact on the legitimacy of the judiciary. Changes in the potential to win are simply changes in the equation associated with the outcome, and they are identified from a largely neutral perspective.

Incorporated in the scenarios is the final important implication that arises from the difference in the two approaches. Not only is the correct approach important in order to offer the best possible explanation of the decision to appeal, but the two different approaches have divergent implications for how we interpret a variety of other behaviors by individuals in regard to the courts, such as compliance and court-related violence, as well as for our understanding of the source of the legitimacy of the judiciary. In fact, in later chapters, I will argue that it is the traditional focus on the outcome-based approach that has restricted the ability of legal scholars to offer a comprehensive understanding of such issues.

Thus, the difference in the two approaches has a variety of important implications. In simple terms, it matters which approach legal scholars adopt in terms of their subsequent ability to explain the behavior of litigants in their decisions to appeal. It matters in terms of the ability of legal scholars to explain the related behavior of individuals in regard to the judiciary, including the important issues of legitimacy, compliance, and court-related violence. Finally, the difference in the two approaches has important policy consequences in terms of how we interpret the acts of individuals and how, should we so choose, the number of appeals could be decreased.

The Decision to Appeal as Seen by Actual Litigants

In this book, I use the actual behavior of losing litigants and the ideas they articulate as the basis for comparing the two approaches. However, rather than attempting to test a variety of hypotheses in order to confirm empirically the dominance of one approach, I am interested primarily in developing the parameters of the two approaches. Given such a focus, it is clear that the current study can make no conclusive claims, but this is no great drawback since the real value of the current study lies in redefining how we con-

THE RESEARCH MODEL

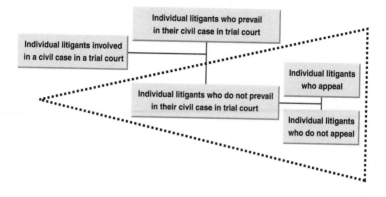

sider individual behavior in relation to the courts in a manner that points the way to more comprehensive research in the future.

The research design focuses only on those litigants who, when faced with the decision whether to appeal, chose to appeal in contrast to those who did not appeal. Since litigants who prevail in the trial court are precluded from appealing, only litigants who lost in the trial court were interviewed. While it may be possible in some rare instances to appeal after prevailing in the trial court, the current research was interested in the response of those individual civil litigants who had lost in the trial court. The research was interested in those civil litigants who are faced with the decision to appeal at the completion of their trial court action rather than those litigants involved in interlocutory appeals during the actual trial court proceedings (see Solimine 1990). Finally, the research was interested in the decision of the individual civil litigants to appeal rather than their subsequent ability to proceed with their appeal; for instance, many litigants express a formal desire to appeal by filing the documents required to initiate an appeal, but the courts reject such requests on a variety of legal and financial grounds.

Using a sample of individual civil litigants who have lost in the trial court, the research is designed to compare the behavior of these litigants and their ideas in regard to their decisions whether to appeal in order to highlight the differences between the litigants that appealed and the litigants that did not appeal. The design was created on the premise that the differences in the behavior and the ideas of otherwise similarly situated litigants should reveal the reasons for their subsequent differences in regard to the decision whether to appeal (see diagram "The Research Model").

The sample involved all individual civil litigants, except those cases in which the selected court restricted access to the files (such as civil law rape cases and adoptions),[4] who had lost in the trial court in four selected court sites. To facilitate the generalizability of the results, the research was designed to ensure that the sample embodied the greatest possible range of individual civil litigants. The research design involved four court sites—three appellate courts and a single trial court—in three very different American states (Illinois, Minnesota, and Mississippi), three very different types of court systems (county court, intermediate state appellate court, and state supreme court), and three different constituencies (strictly urban, urban/rural mix, and mostly rural). The three appellate court sites—the Court of Appeals of the Circuit Court of Cook County (Illinois), the Minnesota Court of Appeals, and the Mississippi Supreme Court—were court systems that had very different local legal cultures (Church 1985). In contrast to the three appellate court sites, Ramsey County Court (Minnesota) was the single court site chosen from which to select losing litigants who did not appeal, and this court was chosen to be representative of a typical middle-sized civil court that dealt with a wide range of civil cases originating from urban and rural areas.

The sample consisted of 1,103 individual civil litigants who had lost in the trial court in one of the four sites (see table 2). Of these 1,103 individual civil litigants:

- 105 were individual litigants who, between August 1991 and May 1992, filed a *Notice of Appeal* with the Law Division of the Circuit Court of Cook County at Daley Plaza, Chicago;
- 421 were individual civil litigants who filed a *Statement of the Case,* between February 1992 and September 1992, within the court-designated category of "other civil cases" requesting an appeal in the Minnesota Court of Appeals;
- 96 were individual civil litigants who filed a *Notice of Appeal* in the Mississippi Supreme Court between February 1995 and May 1995;
- 481 were individual civil litigants who had lost a case in the Ramsey County Court in St. Paul, Minnesota, between April 1992 and September 1992, and who had not filed an appeal within the ninety-day period specified by Minnesota law as the deadline for appealing.

TABLE 2

CASE TYPE AND LOCATION OF THE SAMPLE OF INDIVIDUAL CIVIL LITIGANTS

Category	Type of Action within Category	CC	MN	MS	RC	Total
Administrative review			50		11	61
Civil rights/ discrimination			9		11	20
Contempt of court			1			1
Contract	Property	20	43	11	163	237
	Services rendered		8	5	72	85
	Lawyer's legal fees	2	6		8	16
	Tenure dispute	1				1
	Landlord/tenant		3	1	16	20
	Insurance	1	18	1	35	55
Day care licensing			1			1
Free speech			2			2
Freedom of information		2	2			4
Guardianship			2		4	6
Marriage dissolution	Property/alimony/ child support		103	27	12	142
	Custody/visitation/ legal access		28	10	15	53
	Safety/protective orders		1		6	7
	Other		1			1
Paternity			10	2		12
Probate		1	9	4	14	28
Social Security			1			1
Tax		3	1	1	1	6
Torts	Personal injury	39	36	14	89	178
	Product liability	10	2	2	10	24
	Medical malpractice	11	8	5	8	32
	Other	9	13	5	5	32
Unemployment compensation		3	56	5		64
Worker's compensation		1	1	1	1	4
Wrongful discharge		2	6	2		10
Total		105	421	96	481	1,103

CC: Cook County, Illinois   MN: Minnesota
MS: Mississippi   RC: Ramsey County, Minnesota

TABLE 3

CASE TYPE OF THE SAMPLE OF INDIVIDUAL
CIVIL LITIGANTS: LITIGANTS WHO APPEALED VERSUS
LITIGANTS WHO DID NOT APPEAL

Category	Type of Action within Category	Litigants Who Did Not Appeal	Litigants Who Did Appeal	Total
Administrative review		11	50	61
Civil rights/discrimination		11	9	20
Contempt of court			1	1
Contract	Property	163	74	237
	Services rendered	72	13	85
	Lawyer's legal fees	8	8	16
	Tenure dispute		1	1
	Landlord/tenant	16	4	20
	Insurance	35	20	55
	Other			
Day-care licensing			1	1
Free speech			2	2
Freedom of information			4	4
Guardianship		4	2	6
Marriage dissolution	Property/alimony/ child support	12	130	142
	Custody/visitation/ legal access	15	38	53
	Safety/protective orders	6	1	7
	Other		1	1
Paternity			12	12
Probate		14	14	28
Social Security			1	1
Tax		1	5	6
Torts	Personal injury	89	89	178
	Product liability	10	14	24
	Medical malpractice	8	24	32
	Other	5	27	32
Unemployment compensation			64	64
Worker's compensation		1	3	4
Wrongful discharge			10	10
Total		481	622	1,103

Table 3 compares the sample of 1,103 individual civil litigants in terms of the 622 litigants who appealed (57 percent) versus the 481 litigants who did not appeal (43 percent). As is evident from table 3, contract cases were more prevalent in the part of the sample involving litigants who did not appeal. In contrast, marriage dissolution cases were less prevalent in the part of the sample involving litigants who did not appeal. However, the two categories are largely similar in other aspects.

The sample involved a wide array of traditional civil cases, including contract cases (414), tort cases (266) and marriage dissolution cases (203) (see table 4). The four largest categories of law represented by the sample were contract (37 percent), torts (24 percent), marriage dissolution (18 percent), and unemployment compensation cases (6 percent). Together, these four categories of law accounted for 85 percent of the sample. The remaining 15 percent of the sample is composed of a variety of less prevalent types of civil claims.

TABLE 4
TOTALS OF CASE TYPE OF THE SAMPLE
OF INDIVIDUAL CIVIL LITIGANTS

Case Type	Total
Administrative review	61
Civil rights/discrimination	20
Contempt of court	1
Contract	414
Day care licensing	1
Free speech	2
Freedom of information	4
Guardianship	6
Marriage dissolution	203
Paternity	12
Probate	28
Social Security	1
Tax	6
Torts	266
Unemployment compensation	64
Worker's compensation	4
Wrongful discharge	10

TABLE 5
INTERVIEWS BY CASE TYPE AND LOCATION

Category	Type of Action within Category	CC	MN	MS	RC	Total
Administrative review			2			2
Civil rights/discrimination			3		2	5
Contract	Property	1	2	5	8	16
	Services rendered		1	2	2	5
	Lawyer's legal fees	2				2
	Tenure dispute	1				1
	Landlord/tenant		2		3	5
	Insurance	1				1
	Other				1	1
Freedom of information		1	2			3
Guardianship			1			1
Marriage dissolution	Property/alimony/ child support		11	5	1	17
	Custody/visitation/ legal access		5	2	1	8
	Safety/protective orders		1		1	2
	Other		1			1
Paternity			2			2
Probate		1		2	1	4
Social Security			1			1
Tax		1	1		1	3
Torts	Personal injury	4	5	1	6	16
	Product liability	1				1
	Medical malpractice	3	2	1		6
	Other	1	1		2	4
Unemployment compensation			10	2		12
Worker's compensation		1			1	2
Wrongful discharge			3	1		4
Total		18	56	21	30	125

CC: Cook County, Illinois   MN: Minnesota
MS: Mississippi   RC: Ramsey County, Minnesota

From within this sample, I randomly selected 125 litigants and conducted qualitative interviews with these litigants (see table 5). These litigants were representative of the larger sample (see table 6). Of these litigants interviewed, 95 appealed while 30 did not appeal (see table 7). Of the 125 interviews, the four largest categories of law in which interviews were conducted were contract (31), marriage dissolution (28), torts (27) and unemployment compensation review (12) (see table 8). The percentage of the total 125 interviews represented by each of these categories are contract (25 percent), marriage dissolution (22 percent), torts (21 percent), and unemployment compensation review (10 percent). These four categories accounted for 78 percent of the interviews. The remaining interviews are spread across other civil law areas. The depth of interviews on the primary four fields allows comparisons of the comments of such litigants, while the comprehensive range of interviews allows the author to be sure of validly reflecting the various fields within civil law.

TABLE 6
CASE TYPE OF THE INDIVIDUAL CIVIL LITIGANTS: INTERVIEWS VERSUS SAMPLE

Category	Interviews (% of Total)	Sample (% of Total)
Administrative review	2 (2%)	61 (5%)
Civil rights/discrimination	5 (4%)	20 (2%)
Contempt of court		1 (0%)
Contract	31 (25%)	414 (37%)
Day-care licensing		1 (0%)
Free speech		2 (0%)
Freedom of information	3 (2%)	4 (1%)
Guardianship	1 (1%)	6 (1%)
Marriage dissolution	28 (22%)	203 (18%)
Paternity	2 (2%)	12 (1%)
Probate	4 (3%)	28 (3%)
Social Security	1 (1%)	1 (0%)
Tax	3 (2%)	6 (1%)
Torts	27 (22%)	266 (24%)
Unemployment compensation	12 (10%)	64 (6%)
Worker's compensation	2 (2%)	4 (1%)
Wrongful discharge	4 (3%)	10 (1%)

TABLE 7
INTERVIEWS BY CASE TYPE: LITIGANTS
WHO APPEALED AND LITIGANTS WHO DID NOT APPEAL

Category	Litigants Who Did Not Appeal	Litigants Who Did Appeal
Administrative review		2
Civil rights/discrimination	2	3
Contract	14	17
Freedom of information		3
Guardianship		1
Marriage dissolution	3	25
Paternity		2
Probate	1	3
Social Security		1
Tax	1	2
Torts	8	19
Unemployment compensation		12
Worker's compensation	1	1
Wrongful discharge		4
Total	30	95

TABLE 8
INTERVIEWS BY CASE TYPE

Category	Total
Administrative review	2
Civil rights/discrimination	5
Contract	31
Freedom of information	3
Guardianship	1
Marriage dissolution	28
Paternity	2
Probate	4
Social Security	1
Tax	3
Torts	27
Unemployment compensation	12
Worker's compensation	2
Wrongful discharge	4
Total	125

TABLE 9
INTERVIEWS BY CASE TYPE AND GENDER

Category	Type of Action within Category	Women	Men
Administrative review			2
Civil rights/discrimination		1	4
Contract	Property	6	10
	Services rendered	1	4
	Lawyer's legal fees		2
	Tenure dispute		1
	Landlord/tenant	3	2
	Insurance	1	
	Other		1
Freedom of information			3
Guardianship			1
Marriage dissolution	Property/alimony/child support	4	13
	Custody/visitation/legal access	2	6
	Safety/protective orders	2	
	Other	1	
Paternity		2	
Probate		1	3
Social Security			1
Tax			3
Torts	Personal injury	5	11
	Product liability		1
	Medical malpractice	3	3
	Other	1	3
Unemployment compensation		2	10
Worker's compensation		2	
Wrongful discharge			4
Total		37	88

TABLE 10
INTERVIEWS BY CASE TYPE
AND LEGAL REPRESENTATION

Category	Type of Action within Category	Lawyer-Represented	Self-Represented
Administrative review		1	1
Civil rights/discrimination		5	
Contract	Property	12	4
	Services rendered	2	3
	Lawyer's legal fees		2
	Tenure dispute	1	
	Landlord/tenant	5	
	Insurance	1	
	Other	1	
Freedom of information		1	2
Guardianship		1	
Marriage dissolution	Property/alimony/ child support	15	2
	Custody/visitation/ legal access	7	1
	Safety/protective orders	2	
	Other	1	
Paternity		2	
Probate		3	1
Social Security			1
Tax		1	2
Torts	Personal injury	15	1
	Product liability	1	
	Medical malpractice	4	2
	Other	3	1
Unemployment compensation		6	6
Worker's compensation		2	
Wrongful discharge		2	2
Total		94	31

TABLE 11
INTERVIEWS BY CASE TYPE AND ROLE

Category	Type of Action within Category	PL	DF	3rd	NF
Administrative review		2			
Civil rights/discrimination		5			
Contract	Property	6	10		
	Services rendered	3	2		
	Lawyer's legal fees			2	
	Tenure dispute	1			
	Landlord/tenant	1	4		
	Insurance	1			
	Other		1		
Freedom of information		3			
Guardianship		1			
Marriage dissolution	Property/alimony/ child support	4	1		13
	Custody/visitation/ legal access	1	1		5
	Safety/protective orders				2
	Other				1
Paternity		2			
Probate		2	2		
Social Security		1			
Tax			3		
Torts	Personal injury	12	4		
	Product liability	1			
	Medical malpractice	6			
	Other	1	3		
Unemployment compensation		12			
Worker's compensation		1	1		
Wrongful discharge		4			
Total		70	32	2	21

DF: Defendant   NF: No-fault action
PL: Plaintiff   3rd: Third-party intervener

Of the 125 interviews, 30 percent (37) were conducted with women. Table 9 documents the case type and gender of the interviewed litigants. The project specifically targeted women for interviews in its letters of solicitation; if there were two people named as the joint individual appellant, the letter of solicitation would always be addressed to the woman in such cases. This bias was designed to mediate the possibility that the project would be left with an insufficient sample of women litigants to make comparisons based on gender differences.

About 25 percent (31) of the 125 interviews were conducted with litigants who self-represented (pro se). The remaining 75 percent (94) were represented by legal counsel. Table 10 documents the case type and form of legal representation of the interviewed litigants. Lawyers pursuing their legal fees were removed from the classification of either lawyer-represented or self-represented litigants. Lawyers in such cases are not the traditional definition of a self-representing litigant, which is considered as incorporating lay representation (Ziegler and Hermann 1972; New York State Bar Association 1988).

Table 11 shows the breakdown of interviews by case type and the role of the individual civil litigant in the trial court. Within the 125 interviewed litigants, 56 percent (70) were plaintiffs, 26 percent (32) were defendants, 17 percent (21) were involved in no-fault actions, and 1 percent (2) were involved as third-party interveners. It should be remembered that Minnesota has no-fault marriage dissolution and, consequently, all marriage dissolution and related custody cases have been placed in the no-fault category. A third-party appellant is a party that intervenes into the appellate action, such as a lawyer seeking awarding of fees or an unrelated party who is adversely affected by the original decision of the trial court. It should be noted that the designation of plaintiff need not reflect the party that initiated the original action, since the notion of role in the current usage is based only on the position of the individual litigant at the trial court stage. Some litigants had been involved in conciliation court actions, administrative review, or prior arbitration before entering the trial court. The current table can be taken to reflect only the litigant who brought the action into a trial court.

The research involves qualitative interviews with the 125 losing litigants. Tables 12 and 13 document the various details of the interviews in relation to the individual litigants. Since there were no existing sources of substantial quantitative or qualitative interviews with losing litigants on the issue of appeal and there were no significant sources of supportive data for

TABLE 12

INTERVIEW DETAILS OF THE LITIGANTS
WHO DID NOT APPEAL

Interview ID	Gender	Age	Race	Legal Representation	Lawyer Gender	Site	Original Jurisdiction	Role	Case Type	Case Type: Specific	Date of Interview
1	Man	45	White	Lawyer		Cook County		Plaintiff	Tort	Other	10.29.1991
2	Man	48	White	Lawyer		Cook County		Plaintiff	Tort	Personal injury	11.02.1991
3	Man	56	African American	Self-represented		Cook County		Third party	Contract	Lawyer's legal fees	09.10.1991
4	Man	38	African American	Lawyer		Cook County		Plaintiff	Tort	Medical malpractice	11.03.1991
5	Man	48	White	Lawyer		Cook County		Plaintiff	Contract	Tenure dispute	11.02.1991
6	Man	41	White	Self-represented		Cook County		Plaintiff	Tort	Medical malpractice	01.06.1992
7	Man	42	African American	Lawyer		Cook County	Cook County Tax Commissioner	Defendant	Tax		02.10.1992
8	Man	26	White	Lawyer		Cook County		Plaintiff	Tort	Personal injury	02.10.1992
9	Man	42	White	Self-represented		Cook County		Third party	Contract	Lawyer's legal fees	02.13.1992
10	Man	51	White	Lawyer	Woman	Cook County		Plaintiff	Tort	Product liability	02.10.1992
11	Man	48	White	Lawyer		Cook County		Defendant	Tort	Personal injury	02.24.1992

TABLE 12 (CONTINUED)

Interview ID	Gender	Age	Race	Legal Representation	Lawyer Gender	Site	Original Jurisdiction	Role	Case Type	Case Type: Specific	Date of Interview
12	Man	35	White	Lawyer		Cook County		Plaintiff	Tort	Personal injury	02.24.1992
13	Woman	64	White	Lawyer		Cook County		Plaintiff	Worker's compensation		02.25.1992
14	Woman	36	White	Lawyer		Minnesota	Ramsey County	Defendant	Contract	Landlord/ tenant	06.07.1992
15	Woman	41	White	Lawyer	Man	Minnesota	Ramsey County	Plaintiff	Tort	Medical malpractice	04.14.1992
16	Woman	20	White	Lawyer	Man	Minnesota	Crow Wing County	Plaintiff	Tort	Personal injury	04.15.1992
17	Man	60	White	Lawyer	Woman	Minnesota	Washington County	No-fault	Marriage dissolution	Property	04.17.1992
18	Woman	27	White	Lawyer	Woman	Minnesota	Ramsey County	Plaintiff	Paternity		04.17.1992
19	Woman	50	White	Lawyer	Man	Minnesota	Hennepin County	Plaintiff	Tort	Personal injury	04.21.1992
20	Woman	45	White	Lawyer	Man	Minnesota	Todd County	No-fault	Marriage dissolution	Property	04.23.1992
21	Man	34	White	Self-represented		Minnesota	Ramsey County	Plaintiff	Wrongful discharge		06.26.1992
22	Woman	32	White	Lawyer	Man	Minnesota	Wilkin County	No-fault	Marriage dissolution	Other	05.07.1992
23	Man	38	White	Self-represented		Minnesota	Hennepin County	Plaintiff	Freedom of information		05.11.1992
24	Man	34	White	Lawyer	Man	Minnesota	Ramsey County	Defendant	Tort	Other	05.12.1992
25	Woman	69	White	Self-represented		Minnesota	Hennepin County	Plaintiff	Tort	Medical malpractice	05.11.1992

Interview ID	Gender	Age	Race	Legal Representation	Lawyer Gender	Site	Original Jurisdiction	Role	Case Type	Case Type: Specific	Date of Interview
26	Man	51	White	Self-represented		Minnesota	Department of Revenue	Defendant	Tax		05.13.1992
27	Man	54	White	Self-represented		Minnesota	Commissioner of Jobs & Training	Plaintiff	Wrongful discharge		05.12.1992
28	Man	48	White	Self-represented		Minnesota	Commissioner of Jobs & Training	Plaintiff	Unemployment compensation		05.12.1992
29	Man	41	White	Lawyer	Man	Minnesota	Mower County	Plaintiff	Guardianship		05.21.1992
30	Man	50	White	Lawyer		Minnesota		Plaintiff	Administrative review		05.26.1992
36	Man	41	White	Lawyer	Man	Minnesota	Hennepin County	Plaintiff	Tort	Personal injury	06.03.1992
37	Man	37	White	Lawyer	Woman	Minnesota	Ramsey County	No-fault	Marriage Dissolution	Custody	06.23.1992
38	Man	46	White	Lawyer	Man	Minnesota	Aitkin County	No-fault	Marriage dissolution	Property	06.24.1992
39	Woman	57	White	Lawyer	Woman	Minnesota	Beltrami County	No-fault	Marriage dissolution	Safety	07.13.1992
40	Man	42	White	Lawyer	Man	Minnesota	Washington County	Plaintiff	Contract	Landlord/tenant	07.14.1992
41	Man	43	Indian American	Self-represented		Minnesota	Hennepin County	Defendant	Contract	Services rendered	07.16.1992
42	Man	51	White	Lawyer	Man	Minnesota	Hennepin County	No-fault	Marriage dissolution	Property	07.22.1992
43	Man	69	Asian American	Lawyer	Man	Minnesota	Hennepin County	No-fault	Marriage dissolution	Property	07.23.1992

TABLE 12 (CONTINUED)

Interview ID	Gender	Age	Race	Legal Representation	Lawyer Gender	Site	Original Jurisdiction	Role	Case Type	Case Type: Specific	Date of Interview
44	Man	45	White	Lawyer	Woman	Minnesota	Beltrami County	No-fault	Marriage dissolution	Property	07.27.1992
45	Man	48	White	Self-represented		Minnesota	Commissioner of Jobs & Training	Plaintiff	Unemployment compensation		07.27.1992
46	Man	51	Iranian	Self-represented		Minnesota	Commissioner of Jobs & Training	Plaintiff	Unemployment compensation		07.31.1992
47	Man	53	White	Self-represented		Minnesota	Hennepin County	Plaintiff	Contract	Property	08.03.1992
48	Man	60	Asian American	Self-represented		Minnesota	Commissioner of Jobs & Training	Plaintiff	Unemployment compensation		08.24.1992
49	Woman	59	White	Lawyer	Woman	Minnesota	Ramsey County	No-fault	Marriage Dissolution	Property	08.24.1992
50	Man	34	Ghanaian	Self-represented		Minnesota	Hennepin County	Plaintiff	Freedom of information		08.25.1992
51	Woman	45	White	Lawyer	Man	Minnesota	Seventh Judicial District	No-fault	Marriage dissolution	Property	08.25.1992
52	Man	57	White	Self-represented		Minnesota	Ramsey County	No-fault	Marriage dissolution	Property	08.25.1992
53	Woman	26	Native American	Lawyer	Woman	Minnesota	Becker County	No-fault	Marriage dissolution	Custody	09.02.1992
54	Woman	35	African American	Lawyer	Man	Minnesota	Department of Human Services	Defendant	Paternity		09.15.1992
55	Man	40	African American	Lawyer	Woman	Minnesota	Commissioner of Jobs & Training	Plaintiff	Unemployment compensation		09.15.1992

Interview ID	Gender	Age	Race	Legal Representation	Lawyer Gender	Site	Original Jurisdiction	Role	Case Type	Case Type: Specific	Date of Interview
56	Man	60	White	Lawyer	Man	Minnesota	Commissioner of Jobs & Training	Plaintiff	Unemployment compensation		09.22.1992
57	Man	60	White	Lawyer	Woman	Minnesota	Ninth Judicial District	Plaintiff	Contract	Property	10.05.1992
58	Man	61	White	Lawyer	Woman	Minnesota	Fourth Judicial District	No-fault	Marriage dissolution	Property	10.07.1992
59	Man	33	White	Lawyer	Man	Minnesota	Commissioner of Jobs & Training	Plaintiff	Unemployment compensation		10.07.1992
60	Man	31	White	Lawyer	Man	Minnesota	Anoka County	No-fault	Marriage dissolution	Custody	10.07.1992
61	Woman	36	White	Lawyer		Minnesota	Ramsey County	Plaintiff	Contract	Insurance	10.13.1992
62	Man	50	White	Lawyer	Man	Minnesota	Ramsey County	Plaintiff	Civil rights		10.13.1992
63	Man	39	White	Self-represented		Minnesota	Commissioner of Jobs & Training	Plaintiff	Social Security		10.13.1992
64	Man	39	White	Self-represented		Minnesota	Commissioner of Jobs & Training	Plaintiff	Unemployment compensation		10.20.1992
65	Man	23	Native American	Lawyer	Man	Minnesota	Civil Service Comm., Minneapolis	Plaintiff	Civil rights		10.21.1992
66	Man	63	White	Lawyer	Man	Minnesota	Anoka County	Plaintiff	Wrongful discharge		10.27.1992

TABLE 12 (CONTINUED)

Interview ID	Gender	Age	Race	Legal Representation	Lawyer Gender	Site	Original Jurisdiction	Role	Case Type	Case Type: Specific	Date of Interview
67	Man	30	White	Lawyer	Man	Minnesota	Commissioner of Jobs & Training	Plaintiff	Unemployment compensation		10.27.1992
68	Man	64	White	Self-represented		Minnesota	Sixth Judicial District	No-fault	Marriage Dissolution	Custody	11.03.1992
69	Woman	37	White	Lawyer	Man	Minnesota	Commissioner of Jobs & Training	Plaintiff	Unemployment compensation		11.03.1992
70	Woman	24	White	Lawyer	Man	Minnesota	Hennepin County	Plaintiff	Tort	Personal injury	10.11.1992
71	Woman	46	White	Lawyer	Man	Minnesota	Koochiching County	No-fault	Marriage dissolution	Property	11.18.1992
72	Man	42	White	Lawyer	Man	Minnesota	Hennepin County	No-fault	Marriage dissolution	Custody	11.19.1992
73	Man	55	White	Lawyer	Woman	Minnesota	Department of Veteran Affairs	Plaintiff	Civil rights		11.23.1992
74	Man	37	White	Lawyer	Man	Minnesota	Nicollet County	Plaintiff	Tort	Personal injury	11.23.1992
75	Woman	40	African American	Lawyer	Woman	Mississippi		Plaintiff	Tort	Medical malpractice	03.15.1995
76	Man	64	White	Self-represented		Mississippi		Plaintiff	Probate		03.15.1995
77	Man	56	White	Lawyer	Woman	Mississippi		Plaintiff	Marriage dissolution	Custody	03.15.1995
78	Man	53	White	Lawyer	Man	Mississippi		Plaintiff	Marriage dissolution	Property	03.17.1995
79	Man	35	African American	Lawyer	Man	Mississippi		Defendant	Marriage dissolution	Property	03.17.1995
80	Man	46	African American	Lawyer	Man	Mississippi		Defendant	Contract	Property	03.19.1995

Interview ID	Gender	Age	Race	Legal Representation	Lawyer Gender	Site	Original Jurisdiction	Role	Case Type	Case Type: Specific	Date of Interview
81	Woman	68	African American	Lawyer	Woman	Mississippi		Defendant	Contract	Property	03.21.1995
82	Woman	55	White	Lawyer	Man	Mississippi		Plaintiff	Contract	Services rendered	03.22.1995
83	Man	55	White	Lawyer	Man	Mississippi		Plaintiff	Marriage dissolution	Property	03.27.1995
84	Man	50	White	Lawyer	Man	Mississippi		Defendant	Probate		04.04.1995
85	Woman	60	White	Lawyer	Man	Mississippi		Plaintiff	Contract	Property	04.11.1995
86	Man	30	White	Lawyer	Man	Mississippi		Defendant	Marriage dissolution	Custody	04.19.1995
87	Woman	32	African American	Lawyer	Man	Mississippi		Plaintiff	Tort	Personal injury	04.24.1995
88	Man	54	White	Lawyer	Man	Mississippi		Plaintiff	Marriage dissolution	Property	04.25.1995
89	Man	48	White	Lawyer	Man	Mississippi		Plaintiff	Contract	Property	04.26.1995
90	Man	65	White	Lawyer	Man	Mississippi		Plaintiff	Contract	Services rendered	04.27.1995
91	Woman	52	White	Lawyer	Man	Mississippi		Defendant	Contract	Property	05.02.1995
92	Man	45	African American	Lawyer	Woman	Mississippi		Plaintiff	Wrongful discharge		05.15.1995
93	Man	46	African American	Self-represented		Mississippi		Plaintiff	Unemployment compensation		05.22.1995
94	Man	56	White	Self-represented		Mississippi		Plaintiff	Marriage dissolution	Property	05.23.1995

TABLE 12 (CONTINUED)

Interview ID	Gender	Age	Race	Legal Representation	Lawyer Gender	Site	Original Jurisdiction	Role	Case Type	Case Type: Specific	Date of Interview
95	Woman	57	White	Lawyer	Man	Mississippi		Plaintiff	Unemployment compensation		05.24.1995
A	Man	40	White	Lawyer		Cook County		Plaintiff	Freedom of information		05.10.1991
B	Man	35	White	Lawyer		Cook County		Plaintiff	Tort	Medical malpractice	05.11.1991
C	Man	55	African American	Lawyer		Cook County		Plaintiff	Probate		05.14.1991
D	Man	40	White	Lawyer		Cook County		Plaintiff	Contract	Property	05.16.1991
E	Man	36	White	Self-represented		Cook County		Plaintiff	Administrative review		05.18.1991

TABLE 13

INTERVIEW DETAILS OF THE LITIGANTS WHO APPEALED

Interview ID	Gender	Age	Race	Legal Representation	Role	Case Type	Case Type: Specific	Date Interviewed
1	Woman	29	White	Lawyer	Defendant	Contract	Landlord/tenant	06.08.1992
2	Man	50	White	Lawyer	Defendant	Contract	Property	04.13.1992
3	Man	35	White	Lawyer	Defendant	Contract	Landlord/tenant	04.13.1992
4	Man	53	White	Self-represented	Defendant	Contract	Property	04.15.1992
5	Woman	34	White	Lawyer	Defendant	Contract	Landlord/tenant	04.17.1992
6	Man	43	White	Lawyer	Defendant	Contract	Other	05.07.1992
8	Man	31	White	Lawyer	Plaintiff	Tort	Personal injury	05.11.1992
9	Man	35	White	Self-represented	Defendant	Contract	Property	05.14.1992
10	Man	42	African American	Lawyer	Defendant	Tort	Other	07.07.1992
11	Woman	40	White	Lawyer	Defendant	Worker's compensation		07.16.1992
12	Man	57	White	Lawyer	Plaintiff	Civil rights		08.13.1992
13	Man	52	White	Lawyer	Plaintiff	Tort	Personal injury	08.09.1992
14	Man	18	Asian American	Lawyer	Defendant	Tort	Personal injury	08.24.1992
15	Man	52	White	Lawyer	Defendant	Contract	Property	08.25.1992
16	Woman	48	White	Lawyer	Plaintiff	Civil rights		09.08.1992
17	Woman	62	African American	Lawyer	Plaintiff	Probate		09.29.1992
18	Woman	36	African American	Lawyer	Plaintiff	Tort	Personal injury	10.06.1992
19	Woman	38	White	Lawyer	Defendant	Contract	Property	10.06.1992

TABLE 13 (CONTINUED)

Interview ID	Gender	Age	Race	Legal Representation	Role	Case Type	Case Type: Specific	Date Interviewed
20	Woman	34	White	Lawyer	No-fault	Marriage dissolution	Custody	10.07.1992
21	Man	54	White	Self-represented	Defendant	Tax		10.07.1992
22	Man	40	White	Lawyer	No-fault	Marriage dissolution	Property	10.12.1992
23	Man	48	White	Self-represented	Plaintiff	Contract	Services rendered	10.23.1992
24	Woman	68	White	Lawyer	Defendant	Contract	Property	10.26.1992
25	Woman	58	White	Self-represented	Defendant	Contract	Property	11.13.1992
26	Man	26	White	Self-represented	Defendant	Contract	Services rendered	11.13.1992
27	Woman	40	White	Self-represented	Defendant	Tort	Other	11.18.1992
28	Man	36	White	Self-represented	Defendant	Tort	Personal injury	11.18.1992
29	Man	37	White	Lawyer	Defendant	Tort	Personal injury	11.19.1992
30	Woman	49	White	Lawyer	No-fault	Marriage Dissolution	Safety	11.23.1992
A	Man	27	White	Lawyer	Plaintiff	Contract	Property	11.23.1992

the current models, qualitative interviews represented the best manner in which to inquire into this relatively unexplored area (Bennett 1978; Berg 1989; Denzin and Lincoln 1994). Qualitative interviews permit the exploration of complex and changing ideas by allowing individual appellants and nonappellants to articulate their own ideas of the nature of the process in which they are involved. The possibility existed that quantitatively structured interviews would provide the litigant with a more socially acceptable rationale for appealing than the one that she truly possessed. For example, if a litigant is appealing based purely on a cost/benefit analysis, a structured quantitative interview discussing abstract social concepts, such as justice, might encourage her to agree with these concepts in order not to appear purely materialistic. In addition, qualitative interviews had been used successfully by O'Barr and Conley in documenting litigants' conceptions of the trial court system (O'Barr and Conley 1985, 1988, 1990; Conley and O'Barr 1987) and I sought to replicate such a format in regard to the decision to appeal. Finally, the pretest interviews revealed that the losing litigants felt more comfortable in discussing relevant issues of their cases in an open-ended question format.[5]

The interviews occurred within six weeks of the filing of a request for an appeal, which was prior to any formal hearing by the appellate court. Since the deadline for appealing was the same for all litigants, the interviews with all litigants (those who appealed and those who did not appeal) occurred at the same chronological time after the trial court decision.

The research design called for two different protocols: one for the litigants who appealed and one for the litigants who did not appeal. The protocols were designed to either prompt the litigants who appealed to discuss the factors that had influenced them to appeal, or prompt the litigants who did not appeal to discuss the factors that had influenced them not to appeal.

The interviews, which averaged fifty minutes in length for both protocols, involved twenty-three open-ended questions (see the sample questionnaire page 163) that included the following thirteen standard items: (1) Litigants who appealed were asked to give their reasons for their original court action. (2) They were asked to discuss their trial court action; and (3) they were prompted for further details in regard to their feelings about the trial court action in terms of the procedures and outcome. (4) They were asked about the lawyers' impact on the decision to appeal; and (5) they were prompted to state who had exercised the most influence in making the decision to appeal: the lawyer or the litigant. (6) Litigants who appealed also were questioned to ascertain their level of knowledge of the appellate court; and (7) they were prompted to state any information that they might know or remember about the relevant court. (8) They were asked to name particular attributes of the appellate court that would have discouraged them from appealing. (9) Similarly, they were asked to name particular attributes of the appellate court that had encouraged them to appeal. (10) In addition, they were asked to name one thing that would have precluded them from appealing. (11) Litigants were directly asked about the impact of the cost of appealing on their decision to appeal. (12) They were asked for their demographic details. (13) Finally, they were given one last opportunity to add anything that they chose to the interview. Within these categories, the interviews were dynamic and explored the concepts that the litigants raised in the interviews. The idea was to allow the litigants to tell their stories in their own words.

In addition to the litigants' own statements as presented to me in the recorded interviews, I possessed a summary of their court proceedings to date and, in the case of appellants, the legal request for an appeal. I also spent a substantial period of time observing the behavior of litigants at each of the chosen sites, including their normal interactions with court personnel (judges, clerks, staff attorney). This material allows me to compare the two groups of losing litigants—the litigants who appealed and the litigants who did not appeal—in terms of a wide range of issues in addition to those that they articulated during their interviews.

This interview material is used to explore the two approaches and offer insights into the factors that litigants use in deciding whether to appeal. In presenting the material in this book, it is impossible to accurately reflect the full diversity and nuances represented in the 125 stories that emerged from the qualitative interviews with losing litigants. These stories were full of emotion and thought. The present setting restricts the ability to portray that complexity in a comprehensive fashion (e.g., Conley and O'Barr 1987). Instead, I use two methods to reflect the different ideas that emerged from the litigants' own stories (e.g., Richardson 1990).

The first method is to use several litigants as representative examples of the ideas articulated by their counterparts. These litigants were chosen at random. The randomness guarantees that their statements are neither more articulate nor less articulate than their counterparts. Rather, the idea is to make the interviews more accessible by using "familiar" litigants to represent the statements of all litigants—a few voices that the reader can recognize, as it were, throughout the book. Throughout the chapters, I will continually return to the words of these representative litigants. By this method, I allow the reader to cumulate, over the course of the book, a substantial portion of the total statements of each of these representative litigants in order to reflect to the reader the general flavor of litigants' responses in the interviews. While it is clear that such a method cannot remove the challenge of selection bias by the author, it is hoped that it allows the reader to better judge the overall content of each individual interview. In this regard, I use four litigants as examples: three litigants who appealed—Appellants 37, 71, and 81—and one litigant who did not appeal—Nonappellant 27—to epitomize the ideas articulated by the other litigants.

- Appellant 37 is a thirty-seven-year-old man who appealed a custody case to the Minnesota Court of Appeals.
- Appellant 71 is a forty-six-year-old woman who appealed a marriage dissolution case to the Minnesota Court of Appeals.
- Appellant 81 is a sixty-eight-year-old woman who appealed a contract case involving real property to the Mississippi Supreme Court.
- Nonappellant 27 is a forty-year-old woman involved in a tort case that had proceeded through the Ramsey County Court.

In order to highlight the typicality of these four examples as well as expand on ideas raised in these interviews, I often supplement the ideas of these representative litigants with excerpts from the interviews with other litigants. These additional comments are not designed to reflect every single reference from within the interview material. Rather, these comments are designed to show the various ways in which the litigants expressed their ideas in relation to each point. These comments represent a sampling of the usual responses in relation to the various points. Where there was disagreement within the perspective of the losing litigants in relation to any point, this disagreement has been indicated within the commentary and highlighted subsequently by the relevant contradictory comments (e.g., Ewick and Silbey 1995).

The second method I use to present the interviews is to condense the myriad of ideas presented in the stories and offer an interpretation of the common themes in the ideas that litigants articulated during the interviews. Combined, the best these two methods can achieve is simply to make these interviews more accessible to the reader in a manner that portrays the whole gamut of ideas raised by the interviews.

The Structure of the Book

This book has six chapters. Chapter 2 considers the outcome-based approach, and the three models of that approach, in regard to the results of the 125 interviews with individual losing litigants. It is proposed that the outcome-based approach is inherently flawed in its ability to offer an explanation of the decision whether to appeal. Chapter 3, using the recent scholarship on process by theorists such as Dahl (1979) and Habermas (1996) as well as the procedural justice literature (e.g., Lind and Tyler 1988; Tyler 1990; Lind 1994), creates the parameters of the process-based approach and subsequently compares this approach to the behavior of the losing litigants and the ideas that they articulate in regard to the decision to appeal. In chapter 4, I argue that the process-based approach offers an alternative theoretical basis from which to consider the issues of compliance, legitimacy, and court-related violence. In addition, I offer a new perspective on individual behavior in regard to why people appeal. The fifth chapter reintroduces the lawyer as a potentially influential force in determining the shape of the litigants' decision making. In the final chapter, I offer some thoughts on the close relationship between the two approaches and its impact on the use of the process-based approach as well as the potential application of such an approach to other political arenas.

2.

The Outcome-Based Approach

To date, legal scholars have used three different models—the cost/benefit model, the individual resources model, and the political model—to explain the decision to appeal. Each of these models can be categorized as part of an outcome-based approach. This approach begins from the premise that, in the words of Richard Posner (1985, 8), "everyone prefers winning to losing and winning big to winning small." The logic of this premise seems confirmed by our social values: people prefer winning money to losing money, and people prefer achieving their desired policy to not achieving their desired policy. Notwithstanding the seeming social confirmation of this premise, I argue that the current evidence questions the notion that people are primarily motivated by the desire to win when they make the decision whether to appeal.

The Models of the Outcome-Based Approach

In this section, I depict the current three models of why individuals appeal by using one representative author for each model. In doing so, I recognize that the goal posited in each model is quite generic and there could be many possible variations on it. In fact, the models propose quite fundamental goals as the basis of why people appeal: the cost/benefit model proposes that people appeal because they want to get more money; the individual resources model proposes that people appeal because they want to shape the laws in their favor for political or economic purposes; and the political model proposes that people appeal because they want to advance political goals. Nonetheless, each of the models can be more accurately represented by allowing one voice to present the ideas inherent in that model.

The Cost/Benefit Model

Although the cost/benefit model appears to have existed for many years (e.g., Rosenberg 1965) and many theorists use variations on it (e.g., Atkins 1990, 1993), the most popular version of the model appears in the work of Posner (1985, 1986, 1996; Landes and Posner 1987). In recent years, Posner's publications have emerged as the focal point of the discussion of the application of the cost/benefit model to the judicial system (e.g., Hirsch and Osborne 1992; Barclay 1997a), and many court systems have implicitly or explicitly adopted variations of the model as the means for appellate case management.

This model defines judicial dispute resolution as a commodity and applies a cost/benefit analysis to it (Posner 1986, 522–28, 550–53). The litigants' decision to initiate an appeal involves a rational assessment of costs and benefits. Litigants appeal only if the potential benefits to be gained from reversing their loss outweigh the costs and disadvantages of enacting the existing opinion. In the case of trial courts, Posner proposes a complex formula for settlement versus litigation. Litigation "will occur only if both parties are optimistic about the outcome"(Posner 1986, 524). The formula for settlement versus litigation is calculable based on the fact that monetary awards are identified as the only basis of the litigation.[1] This model has been adopted to explain appeals. Within this model, "judicial services, such as a trial or an appeal, [are] a 'product' that the parties (in the first instance, the plaintiff) 'buy' when they decide to bring a suit or to continue with a suit that they have already brought, and that the court therefore 'sells' to them" (Posner 1985, 7–8). The court regulates demand by raising the costs associated with purchasing court time. The court also reduces demand by establishing decisions that maintain the certainty of the law such that other potential litigants are discouraged from appealing.

Within this model, there are three transaction costs. The first is the cost of the judicial services, which provide an essential service for the state by creating certainty in the law. The validity of a total users-pay system is queried by Posner, because the pronouncements that result from each case act to encourage settlement in the large majority of similar disputes. However, the current nominal fees charged by the appellate court restrict its ability to control demand (Posner 1985, 10–11).

The second transaction cost is delay. Delay acts as a transaction cost in two ways. First, it reduces the efficiency of the parties in quickly resolving their social dispute through the use of judicial services. Second, delay, because of inflation, reduces the economic value of any subsequent judgment. Posner proposes that courts should maximize delay to a level that encourages the use of alternative arenas but does not encourage the use of antisystemic violence to resolve conflicts (Posner 1985, 6).

The third transaction cost is the financial minimum required by the court to establish standing. Standing is the evidence that a litigant has sufficient connection to a case to invoke resolution by a court, and in the current context, it is the amount at stake in financial terms in any case. Posner proposes that the minimum standing has not kept pace with the changes in current dollars nor with the increase in areas of appellate review (Posner 1985, chapter 3).

It is interesting to note that Posner does not include the costs associated with retaining a lawyer as part of the transaction costs of judicial services. This could be because lawyers' fees are theoretically outside of the purview of the appellate courts' jurisdiction (Posner 1985, 9). However, lawyers' fees are one of the primary transaction costs that any potential appellant faces. Rathjen (1978) noted that the ability of a client to pay the likely appellate costs, including the lawyer's own fee, accounted for 16 percent of the variation in a lawyer's decision to pursue an appellate action on their client's behalf. In addition, appellate courts in some American and non-American jurisdictions have retained the ability to manipulate this cost by establishing legal control over the assignment of legal costs, including lawyers' fees, to the involved parties in most court actions.

The cost/benefit model states that a losing litigant should decide to appeal any time that the potential economic benefits minus the transaction costs are positive. In other words, litigants should appeal on any occasion when they have a chance of gaining more financially if they appeal than they stand to lose financially if they accept the decision of the trial court.

The Individual Resources Model

The individual resources model argues that the continuation of a case is dependent on the access to material resources by its initiating party. Galanter (1974) proposes that a litigant with sufficient resources can choose to ascend the judicial hierarchy. The resources of the litigants include their form of legal representation, their court experience, and their relationship to the court system, as well as their financial and emotional support.

The court system is identified as an arena for the resolution of conflicts "in which actors with different amounts of wealth and power are constantly in competitive or partially cooperative relationships in which they have opposing interests" (Galanter 1974, 96). These differing resource bases create two categories of litigants: one-shotters and repeat players. One-shotters represent "those claimants who have only occasional recourse to the courts" (Galanter 1974, 97). Although their claims may have high stakes relative to the individual claimant, they are usually involved in low-stakes cases relative to the court system. In contrast, repeat players, who are usually corporations and government bodies,[2] "enjoy economies of scale and have low start-up costs for any case" (Galanter 1974, 98). Consequently, they have accumulated court experience in similar situations, which has led to the development of legal expertise. This expertise, and their ongoing relationship with the courts, allows repeat players to be more strategic in their bargaining, including the ability to be selective in the use of settlement and trial positions. Repeat players mold precedent at the appellate level to suit their long-term policy needs. By selecting appropriate precedent-setting cases and settling cases that are disadvantageous to their long-term position, repeat players shape the appellate courts' case pool, and through shaping the case pool, they shape subsequently the courts' decision-making process.

Within this model, litigants appeal in order to establish policy precedent in their favor. Litigants differ on the basis of their ability to gain access to sufficient resources to mount a successful appeal. If they believe that the likely result will create a favorable precedent, repeat players should appeal. One-shotters are less likely to appeal because they lack the resources to mount a challenge to the precedent established by the repeat players.

The Political Model

The final model is the political model. Baum (1981, 69) defines two categories of litigants: ordinary litigants and political litigants. Baum's thesis is that the divergent litigant goals postulated by these two categories account for the variation in litigants' decisions to appeal. Ordinary litigants constitute the majority of cases. They are people who "bring cases to court or appeal adverse judgments because of a direct personal or institutional interest which they seek to advance. Whatever the negative consequences of litigation, people see these as outweighed by what they may gain" (Baum 1981, 69). This aspect of the political model parallels the cost/benefit model, but

Baum's version is not as explicitly economic in nature. Within this model, ordinary litigants normally do not appeal. In contrast, political litigants, who also begin their cases in the trial courts, invariably seek appellate review in order to invoke the policy-making function of the court. "Their primary goal is not personal or institutional gain but the advancement of policies they favor" (Baum 1981, 69).

The distinction between those litigants who appeal and those who do not is based on the differing political goals of the litigants in initiating their cases in the first place. Underlying this distinction is the jurisdictional reach of the court's decrees: political litigants seek widespread policy change and require the greater jurisdiction and policy influence inherent in the appellate court, whereas ordinary litigants seek resolution of their conflict as narrowed to the needs of the two (or more) parties in the present case. Thus, ordinary litigation "tends to be terminated at a relatively early stage because participants find it more profitable to settle their dispute or simply to accept a defeat than to fight on. In contrast, political litigants often can obtain significant victories only by getting a case to the highest levels of the system; a victory at the local level may do little to advance their policy goals" (Baum 1981, 69).

The political model is based on the premise that ordinary litigants do not wish to effect policy change within the scope of their lawsuit. Although Baum has trouble defining the number of cases that enter the appellate arena from within each category, there is a clear assumption that the majority of appellate cases involve litigants with political motivations. Baum also assumes that political litigants must fail (in some manner) at the lower court level, or else they would not need to affect policy change through the appellate courts.

Within the political model, political litigants should appeal in order to meet political goals, whereas ordinary litigants are much less likely to appeal. Political litigants should appeal any time they are offered the opportunity to advance their policy preferences.

The Outcome-Based Approach

These three models—the cost/benefit model the individual resources model, and the political model—are representative of an outcome-based approach. The outcome-based approach is defined by the premise that each litigant is motivated by the desire to win, and the approach uses a metric that focuses on the outcome.

The Desire to Win

The models begin from the premise that each litigant is motivated by the desire to win and assumes that every litigant who loses in the trial court is a potential initiator of an appeal. A potential initiator represents a losing litigant who is prepared to initiate an appeal. The premise of the potential initiator is simply that people would prefer to win rather than to lose and that people accept a loss only because it becomes too difficult to prevail. Within the current models, if there were no transaction costs or legal barriers to appealing, each losing litigant would automatically initiate an appeal. Like the losing gambler who has nothing further to lose by being given a free second roll, each litigant within these models would have nothing to lose by appealing if the cost were free, since the litigants can achieve their goals, whether financial gain, positive precedent, or their policy objectives, only by winning their cases. Thus, in each scenario, the losing litigant would appeal if the barriers to appealing were removed.

- Within the cost/benefit model, once the costs of appealing have been removed, the losing litigant has nothing to lose by appealing and forfeits the opportunity to prevail by not appealing.
- Within the individual resources model, the repeat player would appeal based on the assumption that if she appealed every case she could consistently alter the nature of precedent in her favor by appealing until she received a prevailing outcome. The one-shotter would appeal simply because the difference in resources would not have an impact to the same extent in an arena without any financial or legal barriers to appealing.
- Within the political model, the ordinary litigant appeals because she has nothing to lose by escalating her conflict into the appellate arena. The potential for a subsequent change in the policy of the government may be only peripheral to her wish to prevail, but the appellate court would offer her that opportunity at no cost. The political litigant appeals in order to alter policy in her favor.

The premise of the potential initiator is directly linked to the issue of finality, the point at which the original dispute between the two parties is taken to have been resolved. The premise of the potential initiator identifies that, as long as one party fails to win, there is no finality to the action. Since each party is identified as motivated to win and since one party always loses in the trial court, the party that loses is always motivated to appeal. Further, the models assume that in each iteration of a court action someone prevails and someone loses (cf. Kritzer 1984, 1991; Kritzer et al. 1985). Within this logic, finality occurs only when one party can no longer proceed with the action. According to Howard (1981, 24), the dispute can be taken as resolved when one party is no longer able to initiate an appeal, such that "a judicial decision becomes officially binding on the parties because it either is not appealed or is upheld."

The premise of the potential initiator is that, without sufficient barriers to preclude at least some losing litigants from subsequently initiating their appeal, each and every losing litigant would become an appellant. Consequently, the role of each model is to explain the barriers that preclude some losing litigants from initiating appeals. Two identical barriers exist in regard to each model: litigants will not appeal if they cannot achieve their goal or if they cannot hope to win. These two barriers are related, since restricting the ability to win is one means of limiting the ability of litigants to achieve their goals.

Limiting the ability of litigants to achieve their goal relates directly to the goal posited by each model:

- In the cost/benefit model, litigants can be discouraged from appealing by limiting the ability of the litigants to receive more money if they win than if they accepted the decision of the trial court.
- In the individual resources model, litigants can be discouraged from appealing by limiting the ability of the litigants to establish positive legal precedent if they win.
- In the political model, litigants can be discouraged from appealing by limiting the ability of the litigants to develop their policy preferences if they win.

In each model, litigants can also be discouraged from appealing by restricting their ability to win if they appeal. Restricting the ability to win can be achieved by precluding the ability of litigants to appeal or by predetermining the outcome should the litigants choose to appeal. The first method can be achieved by legislative action that eliminates appellate review of certain classes of cases. For example, it has occasionally been proposed by legal scholars that certain types of appeals be restricted (Mueller

1984; Dalton 1985; Posner 1985). The second method occurs when the outcome of an action is predetermined, such that litigants can no longer identify any reason to appeal. This predetermining of the outcome can occur in two forms. In the thin form, the legislature or courts establish an area of law as settled such that the outcome of every case, should it be appealed, is known by both parties in advance (Mnookin and Kornhauser 1979; Galanter 1983). In the thick form, the legislature predetermines the outcome by action prior to any possibility of appeal; for example, if a Westminster-style parliament demonstrates its superiority over the courts by deciding a case before the courts by legislation.

Distributive Justice as the Metric to Ensure a Fair Allocation

The models use distributive justice as the primary metric to measure each individual appeal. The main purpose of the metric is to allow outcomes to be considered in relation to a set social standard for determining justice. Justice can be evaluated using a variety of standards, including equity, efficiency, ability, contributed effort, and a multiplicity of other measures. For example, it is possible to consider the outcome in relation to an individual's contributed effort (Adams 1963), his ability (Nozick 1974), his needs (Husami 1980; Wood 1980) or some other predefined characteristic (e.g., Ackerman 1980; Geras 1985; Benn 1988). While the three representative models are not explicit about the appropriate standard to use in assessing the courts' actions, the models clearly define that justice can be achieved only by each litigant receiving a fair outcome.

These models are also consistent with a notion of distributive justice because they identify litigants as utility-maximizing. Bentham ([1789] 1948) proposed that distributive justice is related to measuring instances in which people maximize their social utility. Each of the current models assumes that litigants are motivated by the desire to win and that they should attempt always to maximize their chosen utility—their financial situation, their positive precedents, or their policy preferences. Since litigants are assumed to maximize their utility in order to achieve their goals and the process is treated as neutral in determining the outcome, the only aspect within such models that is relevant to be measured in order to ensure a fair allocation is the outcome that each litigant receives in relation to the collective outcomes and a larger notion of justice.

The Inherent Flaws in the Outcome-Based Approach

While legal scholars have used these three models, only a few, disparate aspects of these models have been tested by empirical research (e.g., Songer, Cameron and Segal 1995; Barclay 1997a). Instead, these models have become accepted primarily because they support legal scholars' predilection for focusing on court decisions (e.g., Schubert 1965; Segal and Cover 1989), as well as rely on an accepted understanding of individual motivation (Downs 1957). I am not interested in testing each model.[3] Rather, I am interested in demonstrating that the premise that is at the heart of their common approach is flawed and that these models are problematic to the extent that they rely on an outcome-based approach.

In the next section, I contest the premise of the outcome-based approach that litigants are motivated primarily by the desire to win. I show that this premise is not an accurate reflection of the ideas and behavior of litigants when faced with the decision whether to appeal. I demonstrate that the evidence challenges each of the four primary assumptions at the heart of the outcome-based approach: (1) Each litigant should be interested only in the outcome; (2) the process should be neutral in determining the outcome; (3) the litigants can achieve their goal only by winning; and (4) each litigant who loses is a potential initiator of an appeal. In practice, these four assumptions are interrelated, and they flow automatically from the premise that individuals are motivated by the desire to win.

Litigants Should Be Interested Only in the Outcome

According to the outcome-based approach, litigants are concerned with the outcome only. If this is correct, litigants should be concerned only with the eventual ability to prevail. The empirical research challenges such a proposition. One of the strongest counters to this proposition occurs in the case of Palestinian appellants appealing to the Israeli High Court of Justice. Over a twenty-year period to 1987, Palestinians in the Occupied Territories (of the West Bank and Gaza Strip) brought 557 cases to the Israeli High Court of Justice. Palestinians were successful (as in prevailing before the court) in only five of these cases, which all occurred in a two-year period in the middle of the twenty years. Despite this, the number of appeals increased over time. In this context, appellants initiated their appeals in an arena in which their claim had less than a 1 percent chance of prevailing based on outcome only. In reporting this example, Shamir (1991) proposed that the litigants were obviously interested in more than the outcome of their cases.

The interviews with litigants in the present study support Shamir's proposition that litigants' concerns extend beyond the likely outcome of their appeal. Although the chances of winning were higher in Illinois, Minnesota, and Mississippi than they were in the case of the Palestinians, most appellants in the current interviews did not expect to prevail in their appeals. Appellants stated that their lawyers had explained that they had only a very slim chance of prevailing in their appeal. The appellants gave the impression that they understood and considered this advice. Notwithstanding this advice, they still appealed. The following statements from the interviews reveal that most litigants were very pessimistic about their ability to prevail in their appeal.

[The trial court decision] is very difficult to overturn and not confident about getting it overturned. (Appellant 18: a twenty-seven-year-old woman involved in a paternity suit)

I don't think we will win or it will do anything. (Appellant 61: a thirty-six-year-old woman involved in a contractual dispute with her insurance company)

No faith in winning. (Appellant 54: a thirty-five-year-old woman in a paternity suit)

[The attorney] said that usually when you get to an appeal your chances of winning, you know, it gets like we'll say thirty or forty percent. It gets a lot lower. And I said, "What if that don't work and I appeal for it again?" "Yes, you can, but by the time you go to the Supreme Court, it's like it gets rubber-stamped and thrown back the other way. They don't even look at it." (Appellant 37: a thirty-seven-year-old man involved in a custody case)

Not likely we are going to win. Such a slim chance on visitation cases. (Appellant 53: a twenty-six-year-old woman involved in a custody case)

I heard from another lawyer who said "forget it." (Appellant 24: a thirty-four-year-old man involved in a tort case)

The appeals court tend to be very conservative. I think they will rule against me. (Appellant 23: a thirty-eight-year-old man involved in a Freedom of Information Act case)

This finding should not be construed to mean that appellants would not have liked to prevail eventually in their claim, but rather that they had a very low expectation of such an outcome. The opportunity to prevail was also conspicuously absent from most interviews with litigants who did not appeal as they discussed their reason for not appealing. Litigants who did not appeal were much more likely to discuss their perception of the trial court and their expectation of a repeat of their experience in the appellate court than they were to state their expectation of simply failing to prevail in the appellate court.

Overall, litigants gave the impression that they did not expect to prevail if they appealed. This finding is contrary to the outcome-based approach, which proposed that litigants would appeal only in the context in which they could expect to win. While we might not expect that litigants who did not appeal were expecting to win, we would expect that those litigants who did appeal were doing so because they desired to win. The fact that most litigants who appealed did not expect to win their appeal counters the assumption that litigants are primarily interested in the outcome. This indicates the possibility, which will be taken up below, that litigants are interested in more than simply the outcome when they decide to appeal.

The Process Should Be Neutral in Determining the Outcome

According to the outcome-based approach, the process should not be a major consideration in determining the subsequent outcome. Instead, it should be treated as neutral by the litigants because they are interested primarily in the outcome. In contrast, the current interviews indicate that the litigants focused primarily on the process in their consideration of the decision whether to appeal. The focus on process occurred in regard to every aspect of the trial court experience as well as the expected appellate court experience.

Process and the Trial Court

The nature of the process was a major part of the litigants' dissatisfaction with their court experience. All but 4 of the 125 interviewed litigants were not satisfied with their treatment by the trial court. The remaining 4 litigants were satisfied with the treatment of their claim by the trial court. They identified that it had treated them in a fair manner and they could find no reason to appeal. (In the subsequent pages, we will return in greater detail to the paradox that these four satisfied losing litigants present to the outcome-based approach.) In contrast to the 4 satisfied litigants, the remaining 121 litigants expressed great dissatisfaction with their treatment by the trial court. This dissatisfaction focused on three aspects of their treatment. First, the litigants felt that the trial court judged them personally without sufficient knowledge. Secondly, the litigants believed that the trial court did not hear the real issues in their case. Finally, the litigants identified that the trial court did not treat their claim in a fair manner.

Those litigants who felt that the trial court was judging without sufficient knowledge of them as individuals identified the trial court's routine process as removed from the human aspects that they thought were important to their cases (cf. Merry 1979). Merry and Silbey (1984, 160) have proposed that "disputants pursue grievances not only in terms of material interests, but also in terms of norms about integrity, self-image, self-respect, and duties to others." Such a concept was evident in the way that the litigants framed their feelings about how the trial court had treated them. The following statements aptly demonstrate this point.

[The judge] don't care about you as a person. (Appellant 7: a forty-two-year-old man involved in a tax case)

The judge should have been understanding . . . I was so emotionally wrought over that compromise. (Appellant 20: a forty-five-year-old woman involved in a property settlement as part of her marriage dissolution case)

They are really trying to tell me I am lying . . . I am not able to talk. They are putting words in my mouth. The jury does not get a personal feel for you. (Appellant 16: a twenty-year-old woman involved in a personal injury case)

There was no doubt in my mind that I did not want to take it to appeal. Absolutely. If I thought . . . if there was any doubt in my mind that I thought that my husband's death was not job-related, I wouldn't have done anything. But there wasn't even nothing, I mean, and I don't know how they can even judge this man when they did not even know him. (Appellant 13: a sixty-four-year-old woman involved in a workers' compensation case)

This feeling that the trial court did not seek to understand the litigants as people led the litigants to interpret the behavior of the trial court as insulting. They felt that the court was impugning their motives and treating them with disrespect. Such a finding is consistent with Merry and Silbey's (1984, 157) proposition that "ideas about how to respond to grievances are linked with socially constructed definitions of normal behavior, respectability, responsibility and the good person." As the following statements indicate, the litigants felt wronged by the moral implications inherent in the way that the trial court handled their cases.

I was appalled: good honest people treated this way. (Appellant 67: a thirty-year-old man involved in an unemployment compensation case)

[The district court judge] called me a liar. (Appellant 52: a fifty-seven-year-old man involved in a marriage dissolution case)

I have done everything for my daughter and done nothing wrong. I feel I am being punished. (Appellant 18: a twenty-seven-year-old woman involved in a paternity claim)

To be very honest with you, it's like court; it's not like Perry Mason or, you know, a different attorney show on TV where they try to get at the truth. It's basically, it seems like a lot of compromise or, you know, if there's a lot of lies about you to listen to that, uh, and that . . . that hurts a lot. (Appellant 37: a thirty-seven-year-old man involved in a custody case)

Now, I realize that, you know, law is law. But if . . . if man makes the law and then breaks it hisself, I don't think I should pay the penalty for that. Now, that's my opinion. Now, I don't know about anybody else, but I really don't think they should have done me like that and . . . and . . . and just slandered me, you know, and I've been trying to help all of humanity for a long time around here, for approximately around twenty-some years, and I've been on radios and everything and trying to help, and . . . and because I speak so broad, I guess they felt that, you know, I was just one of them . . . as the judge call me, a fox [laughter]. He called me a fox, so when I smiled, the lawyer said, "Look at her laughing." But, see, I knowed I wasn't a fox. (Appellant 81: a sixty-eight-year-old woman who was involved in a contract case involving real property)

I wouldn't do it just . . . I mean, I'm not a person who does things to get even. But there is a question of . . . of respect here for what . . . what . . . there are some respect issues here that . . . that were not dealt . . . dealt with, and they will only be dealt with if . . . if we pursue this, um, and . . . and I'm not even sure the . . . whether the outcome will greatly influence whether my husband respects me anymore for having done this. (Appellant 71: a forty-six-year-old woman involved in a marriage dissolution action)

In addition to the feeling that the trial court was judging them without sufficient personal knowledge, the litigants believed that the trial court did not hear the real issues in their case. There was a general feeling that the primary issue in their case was not among the issues discussed by the court. In a sense, the litigants thought that the trial court had missed the point of the case. Almost all litigants consistently referred to the feeling that the trial court had missed the primary issue as far as they were concerned. There was a general feeling among the litigants that they had lost control of the direction of their court case and the issues involved in it. One litigant summed up this feeling when he referred to the trial court as a "kangaroo court" (Appellant 52). Similarly, as these statements by the litigants indicate, many of them felt that the trial court did not consider the facts in their case in their correct context.

The issue was something else. We did not begin to do what we were there for. (Appellant 67: a thirty-year-old woman involved in an unemployment compensation case)

The issues did not come out. (Appellant 61: a thirty-six-year-old woman involved in a contractual claim against an insurance company)

They don't know the real facts. (Appellant 51: a forty-five-year-old woman involved in a property settlement as part of her marriage dissolution case)

It was as though it did not listen to our arguments. (Appellant 44: a forty-five-year-old man involved in a property settlement as part of his marriage dissolution case)

The issues did not come out. (Appellant 61: a thirty-six-year-old woman involved in a contractual claim against an insurance company)

Why didn't the court understand ? (Appellant 70: a twenty four-year-old woman involved in a personal injury action)

Yeah, because, um, the first time that I went into court, I said, you know, that she's got all kinds of sworn affidavits, and they're supposed to be the truth, and this is, um, when we were separated. And I said if you look at them, we can prove, you know, that she's not telling the truth. And they said to me, you know, "We're not interested in who's telling the truth. The only thing that we're interested in is that you guys don't want to be together" . . . I mean, "that you guys don't want to be together." You know, so it wasn't like they were looking at who was telling the truth. (Appellant 37: a thirty-seven-year-old man involved in a custody case)

Finally, the litigants identified that the trial court did not treat their claim in a fair manner. The majority of appellants considered the procedure of the trial court as "unfair" or "unjust." One litigant succinctly described the procedures used by the district court in his case as "horse shit" (Appellant 6). The following statement reveals the general belief of the litigants that they were treated in an unfair manner by the district court.

I was starting to get agitated 'cause I . . . I do get, uh . . . I do get agitated thinking about this subject, and the more I . . . I feel it, um, the more it feels like injustice I was not prepared for. And I don't know where the justice needs to be, um, changed in order for it to . . . for the system to work properly and protect the places where it needs to protect. (Appellant 71: a forty-six-year-old woman involved in a marriage dissolution action)

Overall, the interviews clearly indicate that the litigants focused consistently on the procedures used by the district court in assessing their cases. One reason for such a focus by the litigants could have been the fact that many of them indicated that they believed the district court was biased in some way in its procedures in regard to their cases. As the following statement suggests, the perception of a bias in the process was an important consideration in how the litigants perceived the subsequent outcome.

For me it was the principle of . . . this original referee [in conciliation court] that we saw, he was rude and he was obviously biased. And even if they had only said "Well, you can pay them half the amount, or a thousand dollars" or something like that, I think I would have appealed anyway, because I felt that this person was very biased in what he did. (Appellant 14: a thirty-six-year-old woman in a landlord/tenant case)

Many litigants attributed the unfair treatment by the trial court to the trial court's bias against them based on some social characteristic. According to the outcome-based approach, the social characteristics of the losing litigants are defined as irrelevant, with the exception of economic and legal resources.[4] The interviews and secondary material do not support such an approach. The interviews demonstrated that the litigants openly discussed the impact of their gender, nationality, education, geographical location, age, and occupation as important elements in relation to their perceptions of the present and potential treatment of their claim before the courts. Litigants often stated that the trial court was biased against them either as a person or as a representative of some social group. When questioned as to why the judge would be biased against them, litigants considered that the bias stemmed from the court's dislike of individual appellants (rather than companies or government agencies) or proposed that the court's bias was against some social characteristic of the appellant (of which gender and socioeconomic status were the most frequently mentioned). As the incredibly wide array of the following statements indicates, almost all litigants identified that the court was biased against them for some reason.

The judge would lean toward the school district. (Appellant 66: a sixty-three-year-old man involved in a wrongful discharge case)

[The judge] was not arbitrary, just in favor of the company. (Appellant 4: a thirty-eight-year-old man involved in a medical malpractice suit)

Wealth has a great deal to do with the decisions made. (Appellant 56: a sixty-year-old man involved in an unemployment compensation claim)

The judge had already made up his mind. He was biased against men in custody cases. (Appellant 60: a thirty-one-year-old man involved in a custody case)

Judge was a feminist. He was biased toward women. (Appellant 43: a sixty-nine-year-old man involved in a property settlement as part of his marriage dissolution case)

The judge was biased toward companies, sees them as a person. (Appellant 64: a thirty-nine-year-old man involved in an unemployment compensation claim)

The judge was biased against me as a person from Iran. (Appellant 46: a fifty-one-year-old man involved in an unemployment compensation claim)

Court personnel were biased. They made statements against women and single parents. (Appellant 69: a thirty-seven-year-old woman involved in an unemployment compensation case)

[Court] is a conspiracy against the male. (Appellant 68: a sixty-four-year-old man involved in a custody case)

The judge was pro-university, ashamed such a case should come before him. (Appellant 50: a thirty-four-year-old man involved in a Freedom of Information Act case)

It was a compromise that the judge thought he was doing, I think, the right thing. Now, I . . . there's two things that I think about that. One is, I thought that there was something going on within his own family, uh, that maybe prejudiced him — [Interviewer: The judge?] — in terms of some kind . . . yes . . . in . . . in terms of, um, some, uh, more financial advantageous award for me. Now I haven't gotten anybody that would find that out for sure. [Interviewer: So do you think he was biased?] If a man was being separated from by his wife, even if it was a judge, and he was feeling some kind of intense emotions at the time because of his own circumstances, I don't know how he could be fairly unbiased in terms of my case. (Appellant 71: a forty-six-year-old woman involved in a marriage dissolution action)

I think he was biased; the fact that he obviously didn't look at the facts. He couldn't have. (Nonappellant 27: a forty-year-old woman involved in a tort case)

Judge was definitely biased. He was very one-sided. (Nonappellant 12: a fifty-seven-year-old man involved in a civil rights case)

A further indication of the important role that litigants attributed to the procedures the trial court used in reaching a decision in their cases can be seen in the fact that some litigants expressed reservations about the parochial attitudes of the trial courts in relation to their local communities. These litigants sought to remove their claims from local political concerns and local community standards. Appellants often expressed the feeling that they were disadvantaged by the fact that their trial court case was heard in the same community in which they lived, and they identified it as an important advantage that the judges of the appellate court were not from the same area. This feeling seemed to be prevalent particularly among appellants involved in contract and marriage dissolution actions. Not surprisingly, this sentiment was more likely to be expressed by the litigants in Minnesota and Mississippi; both sites where the appellate courts' jurisdictions involved a variety of districts situated outside of the normal seat of the appellate court.[5] The following statement captures this feeling quite vividly.

> [My lawyer's] confident and I'm confident that it is going into the court of appeals where we have three judges in St. Paul who have no vested interest. Not saying the [trial court] judge, he's not a shareholder in the district or anything, but he lives out there, you know, it is a parochial community to begin with, and I think he may have some natural biases he may or may not be aware of, but now it is going to be heard in the appeals court in St. Paul where it is going to be heard of the letter of the law and by judges, they got no vested interest one way or the other in the situation. (Appellant 66: a sixty-three-year-old man involved in a wrongful discharge case)

This same sentiment was not evident among the litigants in Cook County, where the appellate court was situated in the same geographical area. It may not have been a major issue in Cook County specifically because the diversity and magnitude of Cook County's population countered such a small town feeling and ensured a sense of relative anonymity in regard to the actions of the litigants.

Process and the Appellate Court
The interviews demonstrated that as well as focusing on the process in terms of their consideration of the trial court, the litigants were influenced by the process they expected to encounter in the appellate court should they appeal. For example, the presence of the three-judge panels in the appellate court in contrast to single-judge benches in the trial court was an important aspect to many appellants. When asked to consider whether they would get

a better deal in the appellate court, almost every litigant who appealed thought they would get a better deal and named the presence of more than one judge in the appellate court as the primary reason. The litigants believed that such panels allowed the appellate court's judges to be less subject to external political or internal individual pressures. Litigants stressed the fact that three-judge panels would lessen the chances of the biases of one judge influencing the outcome, especially as a result of political pressure. As Appellant 5, a forty-eight-year-old man involved in a contractual dispute, noted about such panels, "They look at the record of the case. They are less arbitrary, less subject to political pressures, less worried about their own ass." The following statement gives a little of the flavor of the responses by these litigants on this issue.

> Yes, I think that there are three people instead of one person. [Interviewer: How does that help?] Because I think that if . . . unless they . . . as long as they are interactive they have a chance to use the synergistic effect, which is they review it and they talk about it and they come to a collective decision and some may disagree and some may feel strongly about something. But if they are doing what I imagine they ought to be doing as a team, they will come back with a better consensus and . . . and report than one judge trying to make the decision himself . . . based on only his experience. (Appellant 71: a forty-six-year-old woman involved in a marriage dissolution action)

Litigants who appealed also clearly expected the judges of the appellate court to be very different in experience and learning from their trial court counterparts. They consistently referred to their expectations that the personnel of the appellate court would be more sensitive to the issues in their claim than the district court judges had demonstrated themselves to be. As these three examples indicate, litigants who had chosen to appeal (but who had yet to have any formal interaction with the appellate court) articulated their conviction that the appellate courts were staffed with more learned, experienced judges, who were more intelligent than their trial court counterparts.

> I guess I would hope that the [court of appeals] may be on the . . . the more the forefront of recognizing the contribution of women who stay at home to raise their families as a contribution. [Interviewer: Is there any reason why you would think they would be closer to the forefront?] But if

you're faced with this more often because there are more people talking about it or complaining about it, then the awareness has to be increased. If you are in a remote community . . . and I do not know whether remote communities . . . if there is any correlation between education and isolated communities, that's a strange one, I don't know whether there is or not. But if you are in a community where the means is not there to appeal and the education is not there to recognize a lack of justice and the verbal skills are not there to express it in a small community . . . then to be in a metropolitan area where there are more people with more skills and abilities who are making more noise about injustice and working for changes, then that is what is an advantage and an opportunity for the men in the [court of appeals]. (Appellant 71: a forty-six-year-old woman involved in a marriage dissolution action)

The judges that sit on a court of appeals are probably more learned and would really consider the hard facts of this case. . . . I think I have always had the impression that judges that sit on a court of appeals is a . . . well, let's put it this way, they are a notch above of a municipal judge or an unemployment commissioner's office or what have you. (Appellant 56: a sixty-year-old man involved in an unemployment compensation claim)

[The judges on the court of appeals] are more unbiased, not a narrow view. They are not connected to local community. More sensitive, better trained. They have more experience. It helps to have been involved in other issues. (Appellant 64: a thirty-nine-year-old man involved in an unemployment compensation claim)

The litigants did not merely focus a large part of their attention on the process without purpose. Rather, the issue of process took on two meanings for the litigants. First, they identified that the process itself was their goal in going to court in the first place. For example, although the litigants did not expect to prevail in their appeal, this attitude was offset among appellants because they viewed the appellate process itself as able to demonstrate to opposing parties the inappropriateness of their behavior. Appellants desperately sought to have someone in authority officially endorse their perception of the issues. The fact that the appellate court would treat their claims seriously seemed to vindicate the appellants' perceptions of the appropriateness of their claim. They perceived the appellate court's willingness to accept their claim as either a sanction on the opposing party or a sanction on the district court in response to its earlier negative treatment of them—a point that is taken up in the next section.

Second, the litigants identified the process as related directly to determining the possible outcome. In an outcome-based approach, one would expect the focus of losing litigants' dissatisfaction to remain on the outcome itself, whether they won or lost. Instead, losing litigants focused on a variety of procedural aspects as well as the outcome. Such a focus did not eliminate consideration of outcome. Instead, it defined outcome as directly determined by the process used to create that outcome. Using the analogy of the tossed coin, the losing litigants did not conceive that it was possible for a coin tossed by the same or similar people to lead to a different outcome. Thus, their focus was not on the replication of outcome; but rather, they focused on a replication of process, which they assumed could lead only to a replication of outcome. (This is an issue that will be taken up further in the subsequent chapter on the process-based approach).

Overall, the litigants demonstrated that the process was the major focus in how they perceived their trial court experience. Further, expectations about the process formed a major part of the litigants' considerations of the appellate arena. The process formed the basis for assessing the litigants' experience at every stage. Such a focus on process seems in direct contradiction to the assumptions of the outcome-based approach, which proposes that the process should be treated as neutral in relation to the outcome.

Litigants Can Achieve Their Goals Only by Winning

The outcome-based approach begins from the assumption that all losing litigants would prefer to win. The subsequent role of the models of this approach is simply to define the actual goal that the litigant is striving to achieve. Once the goal is defined (financial gain, positive precedent, or policy preferences, respectively, in the three current models), the motivation that drives the litigants toward the goal is assumed, because the models are premised on the notion that litigants will continue until their goals are met. Achieving the goal and winning the court case are treated as synonymous.

The idea that winning is not synonymous with achieving one's goal is supported by the evidence, which was briefly mentioned in the last section, that the process itself appeared to be the goal that many litigants sought to achieve. Although it is inconsistent with the outcome-based approach, even some legal scholars who adopt such an approach recognize that the very act of appealing can fulfill the goals of some litigants—a proposition often found in the literature on appeals despite a lack of supporting empirical evidence or a theoretical logic for this occurrence (Shapiro 1980, 629; Baum 1994). For example, Posner (1985, 6) comments on the "fact noted by many judges that a plaintiff who loses his lawsuit may nevertheless feel happier for having sued and lost than if he had not sued at all." However, the outcome-based approach has no means of incorporating such an idea.

The idea that the process itself is an important goal for some litigants has two facets. On the one hand, some litigants identified that it was their negative treatment by the trial court that became the focus of the problem that would be rectified by the action of appealing. In such cases, appealing was defined as bringing the litigant's unfair treatment by the trial court to the attention of a more powerful body. The following statements summarize this perspective.

> I want the court system to know what that judge did to me. I was victimized by the court. (Appellant 15: a forty-one-year-old woman involved in a medical malpractice case)

> I was hoping that there would be some stage in the system that if I appealed it, if a judge looked at what the referee said, he'd say, "Hey, you didn't do this right." (Appellant 37: a thirty-seven-year-old man involved in a custody case)

> Appeal process was going to get done to show [trial court] judge he was wrong. (Appellant 29: a forty-one-year-old man involved in a conservatorship case)

On the other hand, many litigants believed that the process of appealing would highlight the disingenuous nature of the other party in a public forum, thereby exposing their hypocrisy for all to witness.

> The case is able to show the bias of social workers. (Appellant 18: a twenty-seven-year-old woman involved in a paternity action)

> I want [the other party] to admit that they were wrong. (Appellant 6: a forty-one-year-old man involved in a medical malpractice case)

> Company will learn about procedures for promotion. This case will teach them. (Appellant 13: a sixty-four-year-old woman involved in a worker's compensation case)

Well, see, I feel like some people are real guilty of what . . . that's . . . if I was guilty of doing that or had did that in . . . in . . . with an intention of doing something, well, probably I wouldn't appeal it either, you know, but because I feel like if, uh, you're supposed to obey the law and keep your liberty if you obey it, and if you don't obey it, cut your liberty off. You understand? [Interviewer: Yes.] But since I didn't deliberately do something like that, and I come through by this unjust law like this, and they plotted against me for other reasons, I believe, and then I thought I should turn to someone else to let them know. (Appellant 81: a sixty-eight-year-old woman who was involved in a contract case involving real property)

I don't want to be forgotten. I want somebody to see I was wronged. (Appellant 16: a twenty-year-old woman involved in a personal injury case)

I guess the chance to get somebody to listen to what's going on because it's hurting the kids, and I want . . . the kids are first and foremost. That's why I appealed it, because nobody . . . there wasn't an evidentiary hearing. There was nothing. We couldn't present any of our side, and there are so many lives within. (Appellant 37: a thirty-seven-year-old man involved in a custody case)

The idea that the litigants' goal were such that these goals could be achieved by the very process of appealing, even if the litigants failed to win their cases, was evident in the fact that many appellants expressed the desire to change something in the system even if they did not themselves prevail. Based on such a feeling, there was a strong notion among the appellants of the necessity that "justice" should eventually prevail, and, as indicated by the statements below, these litigants viewed the process as part of bringing about such change.

I think if there is injustice it takes time for changes to be implemented, and if I can be a part of that process, then that is important to me. I would like to be able to benefit by the process, but being part of the process is the next best thing. (Appellant 71: a forty-six-year-old woman involved in a marriage dissolution action)

That maybe if it didn't help me, it might help someone else, because over the years, my boss said, "Mary, it doesn't make a difference what anybody does to you, you just take it and go on." I thought that for once in my life

I would show you that I will just try. I am not a vengeful person, but I thought maybe some good somehow or other might come out of my going ahead and expressing this to you and letting him know that I did have enough guts to go ahead and appeal it even though I may not get anything. (Appellant 95: a fifty-seven-year-old woman involved in an unemployment compensation case)

That's why I don't give up is because that it can be changed, and as far as we're concerned it's going to be changed. And all this that going on with this case is just, it's not the whole thing at all. In other words, we're going to bring all of this business right up to the forefront every way that we possibly can and we're going to get something done about it. At least that's our attitude. (Appellant 76: a sixty-four-year-old man involved in a probate case)

People don't want to fight the system, just stay quiet. Must fight the system, fight for themselves to force country to change. (Appellant 41: a forty-three-year-old man involved in a contractual dispute over his services in repairing a camera)

Overall, the interviews indicated that, for the litigants, achieving their goals was not synonymous with the need to win. The litigants often expressed a completely different goal in terms of their action. This statement sums up such a perspective by the litigants:

I mean, they'd probably scare me to death. But if [the court of appeals] were genuinely interested in what the right thing is to do, then they would solicit my input and my perspective and incorporate it into their array of information. I wouldn't necessarily ask them to . . . I mean, I . . . I . . . it would satisfy me if they sought that kind of input with open minds and right-heart attitudes. And I wouldn't hold them to ruling a particular way if I felt like they were genuinely listening and genuinely concerned. (Appellant 71: a forty-six-year-old woman involved in a marriage dissolution action)

Such a finding appears in direct contradiction to the assumption of the outcome-based model that every litigant needs to win in order to achieve his or her goal. This raises the problem with the final assumption: if some litigants can achieve their goals without winning, the approach can no longer assume that every losing litigant is a potential initiator of an appeal.

Every Losing Litigant Is a Potential Initiator of an Appeal

The outcome-based approach begins from the premise that each losing litigant is a potential initiator of an appeal. Since one party always loses and that party would not only prefer to win but *must* win in order to achieve her goal, one party should always want to appeal. According to this approach, the desire to appeal is removed only when the litigant either fulfills her goal by winning or is precluded from fulfilling her goal by some insurmountable barrier that effectively convinces her that she cannot achieve her goal through continued court action. The problem with such an approach is evident from the interviews.

Most damaging to the current approach is the fact that some losing litigants identified no reason to appeal because they were satisfied with their trial court experience. Of the 30 nonappellants, 4 were satisfied with their treatment by the trial court and identified their action as completed. Although they had failed to prevail in the trial court, these litigants felt that the issues in their case had been given a fair hearing in the trial court, and they saw no reason to pursue their action further. Unlike the remainder of the losing litigants, these 4 nonappellants stated that they never even considered the option of appealing. This approach was summed up in the following statement of Nonappellant 25, who stated, "Had my say. They had their say. That's satisfying to me." Another litigant proposed that she was satisfied because the "judge was very fair in allowing me to get my story told. He did what he could to help us tell our story" (Nonappellant 16).

Despite their desire to win (as proposed by the outcome-based approach) and their failure to prevail in the trial court, these litigants purposely decided to terminate their action after their trial court loss, because they were satisfied with the process used to reach a decision in their case. The satisfied group ended its action not because it had prevailed but because group members identified that they had achieved their goal independently of prevailing. The fact that some litigants could be satisfied without winning challenges the premise, which is at the heart of the outcome-based approach, that every losing litigant is a potential initiator of an appeal.

Conclusion

When legal scholars have considered individuals' decisions whether to appeal their loss in a civil court, they have approached the issue with the assumption that individuals are motivated primarily by the desire to win. Consequently, when they have constructed models to explain this decision, they have built them to fit within an outcome-based approach. The three dominant models of why people appeal—the cost/benefit model, the individual resources model, and the political model—all share this outcome-based approach.

The problem with the current models is that the empirical evidence challenges their shared premise that litigants are motivated primarily by the desire to win. The four fundamental assumptions at the core of the outcome-based approach are contradicted by the litigants' behavior and the ideas that they articulate in regard to the decision to appeal. This evidence appears to dispute the use of an outcome-based approach.

Even prior to the current research, there was an implication that the approach adopted by the current models was somehow flawed. The existence of examples, such as the British case presented in chapter 1, imputes the ability of these models to explain the activity of litigants in such cases. Similarly, Posner's recognition of the fact that the process itself satisfies some litigants questioned other aspects of his model. Traditionally, these contradictions have been identified as paradoxes, which are usually explained as incidents in which the litigants have acted incorrectly as evidenced by their failure to fit within the dominant approach (Barclay 1997b).

To date, the apparent failure of these models to account for the practical behavior of litigants in regard to the decision to appeal has been approached as an issue that requires only additional tinkering with the models. On those rare occasions when one of the models is tested and found wanting (Barclay 1997a), the argument is that a more sophisticated version of the same model would resolve such problems as are displayed. In contradiction to this approach, the evidence indicates that the structural basis of these models—that is, the very premise on which each model is based—is flawed. Therefore, any model that is based on this premise is inherently flawed. In such a context, the appropriate action is not to continue to use the traditional, flawed approach but instead to develop an approach that appears more consistent with the litigants' ideas and their behavior in regard to the decision to appeal.

In the next chapter, I develop an alternative approach—a process-based approach. This new approach is consistent with the recent discussion among theorists, such as Dahl (1978) and Habermas (1996), that process, rather than outcome, offers a better means of grounding our understanding of the relationship of individuals to institutions and the state. Further, I demonstrate that the approach is more consistent with the litigants' behavior and their ideas about whether to appeal and therefore offers a better explanation of why individuals appeal their loss in civil cases. In subsequent chapters, I propose that such an approach also offers a stronger theoretical basis to explain a variety of individual behaviors in relation to the judiciary, such as court-related violence and individual compliance, as well as judicial legitimacy.

3

The Process-Based Approach

As the last chapter demonstrated, legal scholars have defined individuals as primarily motivated by the desire to win, and they have judged their actions in terms of that predefined goal. In this chapter, I posit an alternative approach. This new approach assumes that individuals are motivated by the desire to be treated fairly. In this chapter, I develop the parameters of a process-based approach. This approach has been largely absent from prior considerations by legal scholars in regard to the decision to appeal. In addition, I explain how such an approach has the ability to explain who appeals and why in the case of individuals who have experienced a trial court loss in a civil case.

The Basis of a Process-Based Approach

The process-based approach has its origins in two recent developments in legal studies. The first development is of a purely theoretical nature. It relates to the meaning that individuals attribute to process. Dahl (1979) proposes that a shared consensus about the procedures for resolving conflicts and demands is the integral means that allows individuals to form common associations. This theory challenges the traditional argument by Downs (1957) and Olson (1965) that self-interest and outcomes are the glue that holds associations together. Instead, Dahl highlights the various criteria that would define a procedural democracy. His goal is to offer a more sound framework on which to base a notion of common groups. Process in such a context is important for more than instrumental reasons; it is important as a goal in and of itself for the individuals involved in the group.

In support of this idea and with direct reference to the role of laws in such a context, Habermas (1996) has offered a process-based theory as a means of legitimating the political system (see also Tyler and Rasinski 1991; Cohen 1989, 30). Like Dahl, Habermas develops an approach to the politi-

cal process that "could at once provide a model of how democratic deliberation should take place and select which features a genuinely democratic
institution should possess" (Breiner 1996, 9). For Habermas, law is one of
the primary means of defining the process necessary to allow the development of democratic deliberation, while simultaneously law is itself a creation of deliberative politics:

> The production of legitimate law through deliberative politics represents a
> problem-solving procedure that needs and assimilates knowledge in order
> to program the regulation of conflicts and the pursuit of collective goals.
> Politics steps in to fill the functional gaps opened when other mechanisms
> of social integration are overburdened. In doing this, it makes use of the
> language of law. For law is a medium through which the structures of
> mutual recognition already familiar from simple interactions and
> quasi-natural solidarities can be transmitted, in an abstract but binding
> form, to the complex and increasingly anonymous spheres of a function-
> ally differentiated society. However, the law is internally structured in
> such a way that a constitutional system, if it is to provide a substitute for
> the integration taking place between the threshold of formal law, must do
> so *at a reflexive level*. Social integration accomplished by democratic means
> must pass through a discursive filter. Where other regulators—for exam-
> ple, the coordination patterns operating through settled values, norms, and
> routines for understanding—fail, politics and law raise these quasi-natural
> problem-solving processes above the threshold of consciousness, as it
> were." (Habermas 1996, 318)

Habermas relies on procedures as a basis for group decision making precisely because process offers the "minimal conditions for discussion and
argument" (Breiner 1996, 10). A necessary precondition for process to function in such a manner is that the process has obtained a consensus, in which
we all agree to the basic rules of the procedures to be used subsequently in
problem solving and we all agree to these procedures for basically the same
reasons (Habermas 1996, 119–20; see also Breiner 1996, 12). The procedures
that we all agree on are viewed as quasinatural because they arise from the
already existing rules established by social discourse and language. In this
form, we develop the procedures for problem solving from shared aspects
that already have social agreement. The legal system is a means to implement such procedures precisely because it offers a form of legitimation of

norms, as well as the means to test these norms in a dynamic social environment. In this context, procedures exist as a means through which we can interpret our role in politics at the same time as it permits individuals to change that role.

Like Dahl and Habermas, procedural justice scholars (e.g., Barrett-Howard and Tyler 1986; Lind and Tyler 1988; Tyler 1988a, 1988b, 1990; Lind 1994) argue that the process used to achieve an outcome can have as much meaning for an individual as the outcome itself. Individuals think about whether they are satisfied with the process that led to their subsequent success or failure in determining their level of satisfaction with their interaction with a legal institution or legal authority. This literature highlights individuals' perceptions and expectations of procedures and it proposes that individuals are interested in the ability to be treated fairly. The focus on process is not purely instrumental in nature. Instead, it serves an important function in defining groups or individuals' status within such groups. For example, Tyler (1990, 174), in developing a theory of why people obey the law, argues that:

> In complex organizations procedures are not used simply to make decisions or resolve conflicts. Procedures specify the lines of authority and social processes that regulate the group's activity, and define the internal framework of the group, just as the group's identity defines it in relation to other, external groups. Because they regulate social processes, procedures are extremely important to the members of social groups. Procedures define social status, access to desired activities and resources, opportunities for participation in the group, and personal vulnerability or invulnerability to exploitation and harm. Because members of the group value their status and security within it, they are very concerned with the procedures used by the group to make decisions. Given their central role in defining status and authority in organizations, it is not surprising that procedural assessments are the key to evaluating authorities and institutions. When people assess their commitment and loyalty to a group they focus on the procedures through which the group functions, not on particular authorities.

According to this theory, individuals' level of satisfaction with interactions are shaped by their perceptions and expectations of the fairness of the procedures used to reach a decision in their case. Thus, Tyler (1990, 178) argues that "people obey the law because they believe it is proper to do so, they react to their experiences by evaluating their justice or injustice, and in evaluating the justice of their experience they consider factors unrelated to outcome, such as whether they have had a chance to state their case and be treated with dignity and respect."

As these various examples demonstrate, a scholarly movement that is interested in reorienting our current perspective on the issue of individual motivation has already begun. I extend the ideas offered in the current discussion on the role of process so that I can use this theoretical basis to develop a more practical approach to the decisions of individuals when faced with a single choice after experiencing an interaction with a legal institution — such as occurs when individuals are faced with the decision whether to appeal after losing their civil case in a trial court. I create the framework of a process-based approach, which assumes that individuals are motivated by the desire to be treated fairly and that they want to ensure that their ideas are heard in a fair manner when those in authority are reaching a decision that affects them. Following the lead of the procedural justice literature, which I discuss in more detail below, I focus on the litigants' satisfaction with the procedures used to reach a decision in the trial court, as well as their anticipated satisfaction with the procedures they expect to be used by the appellate court should they appeal.

A Quick Review of the Procedural Justice Literature

Despite the predominance of procedurally based safeguards in the Anglo-American legal tradition (Rutherford 1992), it is only recently that social scientists began considering litigants' perceptions of procedures (Leventhal 1980; Brisbin and Hunter 1991; Durkin 1991; MacCoun, Lind, and Tyler 1992; Lind 1994). Notwithstanding its apparently ancient heritage, many of the theoretical premises of the modern research in this field originated in Rawls's philosophical treatise (Rawls 1971). Rawls explicitly defined justice as procedural fairness. He argued that, if individuals were placed in a "veil of ignorance" in regard to their future status in the economic, political, and social system, they would choose a system of procedural fairness as the definition of justice. The concept incorporated the notion that distributive justice and liberty would be achieved for the maximum number of individual citizens within the economic and political system through maintaining procedural fairness in the allocation of goods. In simple terms, outcome was to be regulated by process in order to maximize justice. Rawls's theory of justice differed from its utilitarian predecessors, which focused on outcome in functional terms.

A decade prior to Rawls, Adams (1963) posited a direct relationship in terms of equity between procedures and groups' perceptions of outcomes. He demonstrated that individuals assess the level of satisfaction with an outcome based on the procedures used to reach that outcome. Adams's experiments supported the proposition that justice, as determined in this experiment by the level of acceptance of the outcome, was correlated with individuals' perceptions of the fairness of the procedure.

Rawls's general philosophical theory and Adams's specific experimental findings were first applied to a judicial environment by Thibaut and Walker (1975) in an attempt to evaluate individual perceptions of differing legal procedures. Like Rawls and Adams, they differentiated between procedural justice and distributive justice. They defined distributive justice as "concerned with identifying the principles by which anything of value (money, goods, services, privileges, and so forth) can be fairly and equitably allocated among persons and groups" (Thibaut and Walker 1975, 3; see also Cohen 1987). Procedural justice was an evaluation of the fairness of the process associated with the allocation of such goods.

Thibaut and Walker's hypothesis is that "the just procedure for resolving the types of conflict that result in litigation is a procedure that entrusts much control over the process to the disputants themselves and relatively little control to the decision maker" (Thibaut and Walker 1975, 1). Their preliminary research revealed three elements in the perception of procedural justice. First, the ability to exercise some form of *control over the proceedings* was fundamental to a litigant's assessment of the fairness of the procedures. This control over the process included such elements as the ability to participate in the formation of rules and the freedom to choose counsel, as well as some control over the timing and the setting of the decision-making process. Control over the process did not involve a direct control over the outcome, but rather an ability to participate in the determination of the formal procedure. Second, the litigants demonstrated greater procedural satisfaction in cases in which they were able to present their evidence or argument to a third-party adjudicator. The ability to *be present or represented* was integral to the perception that one was being treated fairly. Third, litigants assessed the perceived or potential *bias* that a decision maker might exhibit in the procedure. They perceived that certain procedures, such as the adversarial approach, restricted the ability of a decision maker to display any bias toward either party.

Thibaut and Walker did not eliminate outcome as an element in a litigant's determination of their level of satisfaction. Instead, outcome is only one element among many that the litigant assesses in her evaluation of third-party solutions. However, a limited relationship exists between the process and the outcome. Thus, "although it is conceptually possible for the victor to emerge from the litigation as distrustful of legal institutions, it is far more likely for losers to view the outcome as unjust" (Thibaut and Walker 1975, 67). Thibaut and Walker's preliminary research was expanded by many others, including Lind and Tyler.

Lind and Tyler (1988) developed a comprehensive social psychological theory of procedural justice that assumed that "the experience of procedural justice acts to increase satisfaction and to ameliorate discontent across a wide variety of legal situations" (Lind and Tyler 1988, 75). Using this premise, they synthesized the multitude of disparate research findings in this area and tested these results in relation to the three elements of procedural justice that Thibaut and Walker developed. Lind and Tyler's research has formed the basis of subsequent findings. The underlying assumption of their research was that several core factors were the basis of all the findings in this field.

Lind and Tyler found that Thibaut and Walker's first element, process control, was correlated with other elements of procedural justice. "Process control enhanced procedural justice even when the decision maker was seen as biased, when he or she was seen as acting in bad faith, and when the outcomes were important, but the effect disappeared when the decision maker was seen as not giving consideration to the respondent's view and arguments" (Lind and Tyler 1988, 104). Thus, process control or "voice" was identified as correlated with the litigants' perceptions of the effectiveness of their representation. Lind, Kanfer, and Earley (1990, abstract) subsequently found that "both pre- and post-decision voice led to higher fairness judgments than no voice, with predecision voice leading to higher fairness judgments than postdecision voice." They proposed that voice allowed a person to argue her case in order to increase the likelihood of a favorable outcome, as well as increasing her investment in the proceedings.

Lind and Tyler (1988) also noted that perceptions of procedural justice were dependent on the original expectation of fairness of the individual litigant. Tyler, in an earlier survey, found that "procedural justice effects are weakened but not absent when the individual in question does not expect to be treated fairly" (quoted in Lind and Tyler 1988, 74). Lind et al., in their study of 286 tort litigants, found that "it is not so much the actual outcome or duration of the case that raises or lowers satisfaction and apparent fairness, but how the outcome and duration compare to the litigant's expectations" (Lind et al. 1989, ix; see also Lind et al. 1990; Lind 1990). Stalans (1991, 1994) has subsequently demonstrated that citizens who are audited form complex expectations concerning their upcoming audit by the Internal Revenue Service and these expectations are the basis of their subsequent assessment of the procedural fairness of the process used in the audit.

An individual's original expectation of the fairness of a particular system appears to be relatively robust. A "single negative experience would certainly not undermine your support for the legal system, but it might well lessen it, making it more vulnerable to future reduction if you again encountered unfair procedures" (Lind and Tyler 1988, 83). In contrast, Paese (1986) proposed that an individual's original expectations may not be substantially diminished by repeated negative results. He demonstrated a stability in the defendant's perception of the fairness of a set procedure, which did not diminish despite the manipulation of the outcome. "The subjects' procedural justice judgments show no evidence whatsoever that the procedural justice advantage of high-input procedures was reduced in the later measurements, even though the procedure provided failure after failure to the subject"(Paese, Lind, and Kanfer 1988, 202). In simple terms, if an individual entered with a certain expectation of the fairness of the procedure, subsequent repeated losses did not seem to diminish his original feeling that the procedure was fair. Although this study was conducted in a nonlegal setting, it is supported by Shamir's findings in relation to Palestinian litigants before the Israeli High Court of Justice (Shamir 1990, 1991).

Notwithstanding the likelihood of a litigant failing to learn from a negative experience, the research indicates that once a litigant did learn from such an experience, she tended to transfer that knowledge to her activities in other arenas. Musante, Gilbert, and Thibaut (1983) found that litigants extrapolated their negative experience in one arena to other related arenas. In contrast, Baker and Emery (1992), who surveyed young newlyweds and law students in relation to divorce, raised the possibility that people could hold accurate knowledge of a process but that they could fail to apply such knowledge to their own situation. They found that although these people "have relatively accurate, if sometimes optimistic, perceptions of both the likelihood and the effects of divorce in the population at large. These same individuals express thoroughly idealistic expectations about both the longevity of their own marriages and the consequences should they personally be divorced" (Baker and Emery 1992, abstract). Similarly, Briar found that welfare recipients tend to "dissociate themselves from the image they have of other recipients" (quoted in Katz et al. 1975, 11).

Increasing the knowledge, but not the direct experience, of a person with a process does not appear to lead to more realistic expectations. Baker and Emery found that "increasing individuals' knowledge of divorce statutes through a course on family law did not diminish unrealistic optimism" (Baker and Emery 1992, abstract). Similarly, Raymond (1992, 204) found that "viewers of a televised trial became more knowledgeable about the judicial process. And, despite the fact that they viewed a trial in which a poor person lost to a large corporation, they did not become less confident in the courts nor less willing to utilize the judicial system in the future." In fact, Lind (1991) found that attorneys had a higher expectation of fairness than did litigants involved in the same court, and despite the difference in the level of knowledge, both groups focused on similar criteria in determining the fairness of a process.

The importance of individuals' expectations has raised the possibility that such expectations are related to gender or racial characteristics. In simple terms, African Americans or women may not have high expectations of receiving justice in a court system that until recently sanctioned and upheld racist and sexist policies. Such a proposition was supported by Casper (1978, 242), who found in his review of criminal defendants that race was correlated with evaluations of fairness. Research in this area by Skogan (1989) tends to reveal that fairness perceptions are influenced by racial and class differentiation of the individuals concerned (cf. Morrow 1993). Major, Bylsma, and Cozzarelli (1989) noted that gender differences were apparent in expectations of distributive justice in different contexts. This result raises the possibility of similar gender differences in procedural justice, and Fossati and Meeker (1995) have subsequently found indications of such an effect. Hirsch (1989, 23) found that gender also has an impact on the issues that litigants focus on in relation to the court and found that "women tend to refer to real life events, while men justify their actions and beliefs on the basis of general rules." However, the effect of social characteristics, including race and gender, on procedural justice is still to be definitively confirmed. In a survey of 286 tort litigants, Lind et al. (1989, ix) found that the personal characteristics of the litigants did not correlate significantly with their perceptions of fairness (see also Lind, Huo, and Tyler 1994).

Litigants' definitions of a fair procedure were found to be context-based. "Different procedures maximize different aspects of fair process. Since people do not regard the same criteria as key issues in all situations, they are likely to prefer somewhat different procedures in somewhat different settings" (Lind and Tyler 1988, 110). Gordon and Fryxwell (1989) found differences between closed-shop and open-shop workplaces in relation to unions. Major, Bylsma, and Cozzarelli (1989) noted that there were different expectations associated with gender in regard to work and relationships.

Finally, Lind and Tyler (1988) postulated a direct relationship between the perceived fairness of a procedure and the compliance of a losing party with a third-party-determined solution. Their argument was based on a prior research project by McEwen and Maiman (1984). McEwen and Maiman attributed the relative willingness of losing parties to comply with a small claims court's decision to the litigants' perceptions that the outcome had resulted from a fair process (cf. Wissler 1995). This finding has been given added support by additional research by Poythress (1994) in regard to the decision making of mental health professionals.

In the next section, I take the disparate findings of the procedural justice literature and develop a simple framework that highlights the primary assumptions of a process-based approach. And as I shall show later in this chapter, such an approach is consistent with the ideas articulated by individual litigants as well as with their behavior in regard to the decision whether to appeal.

The Primary Assumptions of a Process-Based Approach

Based on the findings in the procedural justice literature, as well as Habermas's proposal that process is accorded a meaning in its own right by individuals, it is possible to cobble together an approach that highlights the positive role of procedures in shaping the decisions of individuals to appeal. In developing the basis of such an approach, I extrapolate from the ideas developed by the procedural justice literature. Thus, the following delineation of the primary assumptions of a process-based approach is my own attempt to develop a coherent image of the ideas of this literature as they apply in the current context.

According to this literature, a process-based approach begins from the idea that losing litigants are interested primarily in the question of the process used in the resolution of their disputes. This approach assumes that each litigant is motivated by the desire to be treated fairly. Each litigant's goal is to have the issues that he defines as most salient to his dispute treated fairly by the decision maker in order that his perspective on the issues might be considered appropriately when the decision maker is reaching a decision that affects him.

A process-based approach recognizes that the process involves a decision maker whose role entails reaching a decision in the litigants' cases in a manner that resolves their disputes. The litigants enter the courts in the first place in order to resolve a dispute (Merry 1979; Felstiner, Abel, and Sarat 1980-81; Galanter 1983; Merry and Silbey 1984), and according to the process-based approach, the role of the decision maker is to take into consideration the ideas of the involved parties in crafting a decision that resolves this dispute. The role of the decision maker is important, because the process-based approach assumes that the litigant is not interested in directly determining the final outcome; to directly determine the outcome would violate the assumption that the litigant is motivated primarily by the desire to be treated fairly (Thibaut and Walker 1975; Lind and Tyler 1988). Instead, the litigants seek to have the issues that both parties raise considered fairly as part of the process that the decision maker uses in reaching a final decision in their disputes (Lind and Tyler 1988; Tyler 1990). Thus, within this approach, it is the decision maker, rather than the litigant, who determines the final decision.

While the process-based approach does not question the right of the decision maker to make the final decision, it does seek to ensure that the elements that are considered by him in reaching the final decision are consistent with the context of the decision-making arena. For example, it would be considered incongruous for a student's height to be the defining characteristic used by a decision maker to determine his or her grade in a calculus test, but a student's height might be considered an appropriate defining characteristic to be used by a decision maker in choosing a student as a member of a basketball team. In the context of the legal arena, it is assumed that legal criteria, such as the strength of evidence, the legal precedents relevant to the particular issue, and some notion of justice, will be considered as part of the process used in reaching a final decision.

In addition to the emphasis placed on the role of the decision maker, the litigants also play an important role in this approach because they define what the salient issues in their disputes are. If individuals invoke the legal system in order to seek redress for the way they have been treated by other parties, what these individuals identify as the issues requiring redress matters. Any court response that does not address the issues that the litigants identify as preeminent in their dispute will be defined as failing to resolve their original dispute. In addition, litigants also define when they consider the decision as resolving their dispute. The dispute can be resolved only by a decision that satisfies the original parties such that they accept the decision as effectively addressing the source of the dispute. One reason why the litigants might be so eager to be taken seriously by the court in reaching a final decision is because the litigants themselves must live with the subsequent decision.

Within the process-based approach, litigants appeal because, even if they think that the issues in their dispute were not heard in a fair manner by the trial court, they believe that these same issues will receive a fairer reception in the appellate court. Unlike the outcome-based approach, which assumes that litigants can meet their desired goal only by winning, the process-based approach rejects the notion that litigants need to win in order to achieve their goals. If the litigant perceives that her ideas about the dispute have been heard fairly by someone in authority such that her ideas are given due consideration in reaching an outcome, she has achieved her goal even if the subsequent outcome is negative. Therefore, each losing litigant can no longer be identified as a potential initiator of an appeal, because those litigants who are satisfied with the process used to reach an outcome will not appeal, independent of the subsequent outcome. In addition, the process-based approach assumes that only those litigants who expect to be treated fairly in the appellate court are likely to appeal, while any litigant who is convinced that she will not be treated fairly in the appellate court is unlikely to appeal.

The Process-Based Approach as It Applies to the Decision to Appeal

In this section, I develop the outline of the process-based approach as it might apply to the decision to appeal. I am not interested in definitively testing the process-based approach. Rather, I wish to develop such an approach and demonstrate its ability to offer a better potential explanation than the existing outcome-based approach of the ideas articulated by litigants about the decision to appeal. I recognize that there are many other possible variants on a process-based approach that could equally be created using the same parameters, which might also be consistent with the ideas articulated by the litigants.

In order to understand the decision to appeal, the process-based approach focuses on the litigants' satisfaction with the procedures used to reach a decision in the trial court, as well as their anticipated satisfaction with the procedures they expect to be used by the appellate court should they appeal. Therefore, in creating a process-based approach, I develop indicators to measure the impact of various aspects of the process on the litigants' perceptions of their trial court experience, as well as their expectations about any potential appellate court interactions. I propose that there are four such primary indicators. These four indicators are: (1) litigants' expectations of the validity of the legal arena as a resolver of disputes; (2) litigants' satisfaction with the trial court experience; (3) the nature of the litigants' claims; and (4) the litigants' conception of the appellate process.

The elements in the current model are based partially on the procedural elements highlighted by respondents in *The Public Image of Courts: Highlights of a National Survey of the General Public, Judges, Lawyers and Community Leaders* (Yankelovich, Skelly, and White 1977). This study found that three factors (the type of case, the role one played in court, and the process and outcome of the case) influenced litigants' court experiences. In the current model, the type of case has been defined as the nature of the claim, in an attempt to incorporate more than the legal definition of the case. The role played in court has been expanded to incorporate the perceptions and expectations of the litigant regarding prior and future court experiences and subsumed as a guiding definition of the approach. Reactions to the process and outcome have been reintroduced in terms that are more consistent with the present distinction between outcome and process: litigants' satisfaction with the trial court experience and their conceptions of the appellate process. The decision to involve oneself in a civil action as a defendant or to initiate such an action as a plaintiff involves a certain degree of acceptance that the courts have the ability to resolve the original dispute. Therefore, one other element has been introduced: the litigant's expectations of the validity of the legal arena.

Litigants' Expectations of the Validity of the Legal Arena

The Decision to Use the Court

Any potential litigant has a choice of whether to use the court. This choice follows directly from what the litigant thinks about the court as an appropriate site to resolve her dispute: a litigant could accept or reject the use of the court system to resolve legal disputes. If the litigant rejects the use of the court system, there are two options. The person could simply choose to ignore the court system (see Merry 1979; Felstiner, Abel, and Sarat 1980–81) or she could create an alternative system and place her allegiance with the opinions of the alternative system (see Garth 1992; Dezalay and Garth 1995). In each of these two courses of action, the litigant rejects the authority or legitimacy of the court to resolve her dispute. Although she could be drawn into civil court proceedings as a defendant, a person who rejects the authority or legitimacy of the court to resolve her dispute is unlikely to consequently initiate an appellate action as long as she maintains this attitude.

The research does indicate two categories of litigants who might fit such an attitude. Litigants in both categories were more likely to be defendants than plaintiffs. There is no indication among such litigants of any major consideration of the option of appealing. The first category involves those litigants who simply refused to recognize that they could be a part of any court action that involved them personally. These litigants recognized that a case was occurring but refused to legitimate this case by acknowledging that it involved them as a party. Since they believed they had committed no wrong, these litigants also presumed they could not be involved in any type of legal case. One litigant stated that he "did not go to court because I did not think there was a case against me" (Nonappellant 21; see also Nonappellant 29). These litigants simply refused to think about the court case, and they seemed to believe that it would eventually disappear.

The second category reflects those nonappellants who resolved their claim by alternative means. Violence, exiting, and noncompliance were popularly mentioned and used options among some of the losing litigants. Van Koppen and Malsch (1991) have proposed that many civil litigants, despite their earlier losses in the trial court, do in fact "win" by their subsequent acts of noncompliance (see also Wheeler et al. 1987). In the current sample, many losing litigants sought methods of noncompliance, including moving to other states. One losing litigant, whom I successfully tracked down through a series of addresses in several distant states, simply argued,

"Why appeal when we can just sit here and not pay it" (Nonappellant 19: a thirty-eight-year-old woman involved in a contractual dispute). Other losing litigants discussed the possibility of simply filing for bankruptcy if their court actions were unsuccessful in order to avoid paying the opposing party. Such losing litigants seemed to take pride in their ability not to comply with the decision and felt that it punished the other party. Similarly, the current interviews included some statements of violent intentions directed toward the opposing parties. Merry (1979) proposed that violence was often a ready alternative to court-based dispute resolution. A minority of subjects referred to this option as an alternative to appeal. For example, one appellant proposed that murdering his ex-wife could become his only alternative to appealing his case (Appellant 68), and several others discussed equally socially undesirable options.

In contrast to those litigants who rejected the ability of the legal system to resolve their claims, a litigant might choose to continue to use the courts to resolve her dispute for two reasons (see Moore 1978; Scott 1985, 1990). It is possible that a litigant's continued use of the courts is simply a means to challenge their overall legitimacy. In contrast, a litigant could simply accept the role of the court and demonstrate her acceptance through the continued use of the court system to resolve her claim. The interviews appear to involve litigants primarily in the second category. Neither of these two perspectives preclude appealing as an option, but the goal of the litigant differs substantially between these two categories.

Learning from the Trial Court Experience. The litigant's expectations of the legal arena could also be important to the degree that they preclude or diminish the litigant's subsequent ability to learn from her trial court experience. MacCoun et al. (1988), in their study of 286 tort litigants, found that "it is not so much the actual outcome or duration of the case that raises or lowers satisfaction and apparent fairness, but how the outcome and duration compare to the litigant's expectations" (quoted in Lind et al. 1989, ix; see also Stalans 1991, 1994). In simple terms, it is possible that a litigant's original expectations of the behavior of the legal system are so robust that the litigant does not learn from her own trial court experience.

There is a definite paradox between the negative expectations of the court system in general that are held by most litigants and the positive expectations that some of these same litigants hold about the appellate court. For example, the appellants had a high expectation of receiving justice in the legal system, but they simultaneously held a low expectation of the ability of the court system in general to deliver justice. In contrast, nonappellants seemed to start with a relatively negative conception of the courts in general, and this view seemed to be confirmed by the district court's treatment of them. In simple terms, they perceived themselves as "meat for the meat grinder" (Nonappellant 4: a fifty-three-year-old man involved in a contractual dispute). Thus, the interviews reveal that the expectations of the litigants do seem to affect their subsequent behavior. However, the original expectations seem to have a mixed result; that is, mitigating the impact of the trial court experience for appellants while confirming the impact of the trial court experience for nonappellants.

Litigants' Satisfaction with Their Trial Court Experience

According to the procedural justice literature, a litigant who receives a negative outcome, but perceives that the procedures used to reach the decision were fair, is more likely to accept the negative outcome (e.g., Adler, Hensler, and Nelson 1983; Tyler 1984). Thus, the "damage" of a negative outcome is strongly mitigated by the litigant's acceptance of the procedure as fair. In the present study, 4 litigants clearly demonstrated that they were satisfied with the procedures used by the court, and these same 4 litigants accepted the negative outcome of the case with much less reticence than their counterparts. Although they had failed to prevail in the trial court, these litigants felt that the issues in their case had been given a fair hearing. They saw no reason to pursue their action. Unlike the remaining 121 litigants interviewed, these 4 litigants stated that they had never even considered the option of appealing. This finding is in keeping with research by McEwen and Maiman (1984; cf. Wissler 1995), which found that litigants who were satisfied by the original court's procedure accepted their loss.

The remaining 121 losing litigants could be characterized as negative on outcome, as well as dissatisfied with the trial court procedures. Yet litigants receiving a negative outcome *and* perceiving that the procedures used to arrive at that outcome were unfair composed both the litigants who were *most* likely to appeal and the litigants who were *least* likely to appeal. Therefore, satisfaction with the trial court experience appears to be Janus-faced,[1] with the added proviso that the face you see depends on what you are expecting of the appellate court. Thus, their different behavior results from their subsequent conceptions of the appellate court; an issue that will be explored later in this chapter.

The Nature of the Claim

Each litigant enters the legal arena to resolve a dispute, and this dispute is shaped by the legal arena into a claim (Felstiner, Abel and Sarat 1980-1981; Atleson 1989; Durkin 1991). A litigant's claim can be reduced to three interrelated elements: the legal system's definition of the issues, the litigant's own definition of the salient issues, and the litigant's perception of the involved audience she seeks to satisfy by resolving her claim.

The Legal System's Definition of the Issues
Although the litigants clearly identified the legal issues in their case when asked during the interviews, they rarely described their case in these terms. Instead, most litigants appeared to use the legal terms or referred to statutes only as a way of demonstrating to the interviewer that they knew what the legal definition of their case was. One important point to note is that the court records of those litigants who did not appeal reflected a certain lack of clarity in the appropriate legal issues involved in the claims, and such litigants demonstrated a slightly higher likelihood than appellants of crossing areas of law within their claims.

Litigants' Definition of the Issues. The interviews confirm that the litigants maintained an independent assessment of the nature of their dispute; a claim consistent with the current literature (see Rosenthal 1974; Cain 1979; Olson 1984; Griffiths 1986; Felstiner and Sarat 1986, 1988, 1989; Sarat and Felstiner 1995). Only two groups—self-representing litigants and litigants in civil rights cases—appeared to adopt the legal definition of their case as a major part of their own perspective. Self-representing litigants, who represented themselves rather than using legal counsel, were the most likely to identify their cases based predominantly on the legal issue. This latter effect might occur because self-representing litigants internalize the legal definitions as part of their own perspective (see Zeigler and Hermann 1972; Robbins and Herman 1976). Litigants involved in civil rights cases or discrimination cases were also more likely to identify the issues in their cases in a manner that paralleled the legal issues as defined by the court records. One explanation is that civil rights have been popularly defined by their legal definitions in a manner that other categories have not been so defined. For example, it seems hard to conceive of segregation in schools without using legally defined concepts, whereas it might be easier to maintain a separate perspective on a car crash than the legal definition offered by torts.

Notwithstanding these two groups, the interviews confirm that the remaining losing litigants maintained their own definition of the salient issues in their case. Further, most litigants believed that the district court did not deal with such issues in hearing their case. The litigants made a clear distinction between the issues about which the district court were concerned and those issues that the litigants felt were most salient in their cases. In addition, the decision of the trial court did not seem to change the litigants' views of the important issues in their cases. Notwithstanding district court or bureaucratic review opinions to the contrary, litigants remained steadfast in their perception of the important issues in their cases. They wanted the court to deal with these issues even if they were not the legal issues before the court, and they sought affirmation of their perception of the important issues.

All of the interviews, except the 4 satisfied losing litigants, indicate that if the litigants thought they were in the right before they began their trial court action, the negative decision of the trial court did nothing to sway their opinion. In some cases, it almost seemed to consolidate their belief. Similarly, the litigants' view of the primary issue did not seem to be changed by the trial court's focus on some other issue as the primary one. The latter was viewed by the litigants as the trial court missing the most salient issue in the claim.

This distinction between the legal issues in the claim as defined by the trial court and lawyers and the litigant's own perception of the salient issues in the claim has important consequences for the litigant's subsequent assessment of whether the trial court has successfully resolved her dispute. Take the example of a woman involved in a marriage dissolution case. She may define the "real" issue in this case as the sanctioned role of women in our society rather than simply divorce. Since it reflects differences in the very conception of the dispute that the litigant is seeking to have the court resolve, such a difference is more than a difference in nomenclature. Regardless of the decision by the trial court in her case, the failure on the part of the court to address such issues will leave the litigant with the feeling that her dispute remains unresolved until such issues are addressed. As noted, many litigants expressed the feeling that the trial court had not addressed the real issues in their claim and consequently felt that their dispute remained unresolved.

In contrast, those litigants who appealed expected the appellate court to be better able to focus on the real issues in the cases; that is, the judges would be less constrained by the legal bureaucracy and more capable of considering wider social issues in reaching a decision. This idea was well represented in many of the litigants' comments as presented in the last chapter, and it was clearly visible in the comments of the vast majority of litigants. For example, the following three statements by Appellant 81 (a sixty-eight-year-old woman who was involved in a contract case involving real property) are quite telling about the litigants' views of the appellate court:

> I really don't know a lot about the Mississippi Supreme Court, no more than I know that's the place you appeal when things are not exactly right, because I feel like they would do justice by listening to the situation and straightening it out. That's all I know. I thought that that's what they were for.
>
> So I feel like supreme court should be the place to go to, you know, get things straightened out. That's my opinion. I don't know what the law do, but I think they should straighten — and they should be more concerned about society.
>
> [Interviewer: Is there any reason why you think they're more just?] Because they supposed to be over the rest, you know. It's just like anything else. Just like if you work for somebody, the boss man is supposed to know the most, you know, is supposed to know what can be done and what should be done and what shouldn't be done.

In contrast, those litigants who did not appeal reported the feeling that the real issues in their claim had not been resolved. However, they were unlikely to subsequently identify the appellate court as more likely to consider such issues if they appealed. This turned out to be a primary difference between those litigants who appealed and those litigants who did not appeal. This difference relates to the litigants' conception of the appellate court, which will be considered in depth later in this chapter.

Audience. There is one final aspect of the nature of the claim that the interviews raise. The litigant's definition of a successful resolution depends on the audience that the litigant seeks to satisfy (Mather and Yngvesson 1980–81). The audience represents those people with a vested interest in the result of the case, as well as those with some form of direct influence over the litigant. The perception of audience was relatively distant for most litigants; for example, some appellants spoke of the audience as women in general rather than their families or friends. The following example is indicative of the manner in which litigants defined the audience of their actions:

> I am funding issue for other women. The result no longer affects one it was written for. (Appellant 39: a fifty-seven-year-old woman involved in a marriage dissolution case).

While one would expect a Linda Brown to view her audience as other African American children or African Americans in general,[2] we might be more surprised to find such an approach evident in regard to unemployment compensation, torts, or divorce cases. Yet the interviews reveal a similar perspective by litigants involved in such cases. Within this context, litigants identified their audience based on social characteristics, such as race, gender, class, nationality, and political status. For example, many women involved in marriage dissolution cases identified their case as promoting the rights of women. Workers involved in wrongful discharge or unemployment compensation cases identified such cases as punishing companies. Throughout the interviews, litigants identified the involvement of a wider audience as one of the primary reasons for appealing, and it should be noted that the perception of a defined audience occurs almost exclusively within the comments of litigants who appealed. These litigants sought to have the principle prevail even if their individual case failed. These litigants identified themselves as representatives of a group. They sought to have the group prevail in the long run and hoped that the audience would gratefully note their attempt to change the policy.

Litigants' Conception of the Appeals Court

When confronted with the possibility of actually entering into the appellate arena, litigants evaluate the appellate court's attributes and behavior to develop a conception of the appellate court in order to know what to expect should they decide to appeal. This conception of the appellate court forms an influential part in their subsequent decision whether to initiate an appeal, and the interviews confirm that all of the 125 litigants, except the 4 satisfied losing litigants, possessed such a conception of the appellate court. The 4 satisfied litigants expressed very little interest in the appellate court; they defined it as irrelevant to their situation because they were already satisfied with how their case had progressed in the trial court. In the case of the 4 satisfied litigants, it was more than that they were now indifferent to the appellate court. Rather, they had no conception of what the appellate court would be like if they chose to appeal.

In creating their conception of the appellate court, the litigants used their trial court experience as a means to gain insight into the expected behavior and attributes of the appellate court. There are two such perspectives: the appellate court as different from the trial court and the appellate court as a replication of the trial court. Litigants who appealed were more likely to have the former perspective, whereas litigants who did not appeal were more likely to have the latter perspective. The litigants considered the appellate court from the perspective of how the attributes of the appellate court might rectify the problems in the trial court that, from the perspective of the litigant, caused the litigant to be treated in such a poor manner. Thus, the problems in the trial court shaped the parameters for considering the appellate court.

The interviews suggest that the litigants' expectations of their level of satisfaction with any appellate-level experience shaped their subsequent decision whether to appeal. Notwithstanding the 4 satisfied losing litigants, who could not identify any reason to appeal, the remaining losing litigants, based on their statements and ideas, could be divided into three groups. These groups were determined by the litigants' conceptions of the appellate court. In turn, these three groups reflected the likelihood of litigants subsequently appealing; that is, the three different conceptions of the appellate court determined the subsequent likelihood of initiating an appeal.

The first group contained those losing litigants who expected the appellate court to duplicate their recent lower court action in a manner that could lead only to the same result. This group was the least likely to appeal because, based on their belief that the appellate court would merely replicate the trial court experience, they saw no reason to repeat their negative trial court experience in the appellate arena. Interestingly, this group of litigants expected to receive a negative outcome if they appealed, but that expectation arose from their assessment of the process to be used in the appellate court. Using the coin analogy, the first group did not conceive that it was possible for a coin tossed by the same or similar people to lead to a different outcome. Thus, their focus was not directly on the replication of outcome, but rather they focused on a replication of process, which they assumed could lead only to a replication of outcome.

This group of litigants can be contrasted with the second group, which was more likely to appeal. It was composed of those litigants who had a slightly more positive conception of the appellate court. Within this group, the litigants identified the *potential* that the appellate court would not duplicate their lower court experience and in fact proposed that the appellate court offered them the *possibility* of prevailing. There were only 8 such losing litigants in the sample, and they were more likely to be litigants who had been involved in unemployment compensation cases. The litigants who were in this second group had usually been involved in a series of bureaucratic reviews, with changing prevailing parties, prior to their entry into the courts. This prior process seems to have alerted them to the possibility of prevailing even though the situation appears to be duplicated at each level of review. Returning to the coin analogy, this second group believed that another toss of the coin by different people had a great potential for a different outcome. Unlike their counterparts, these litigants focused on differences in the process that they believed had the potential to lead to a difference in the subsequent outcome. There were very few such litigants with this conception, but all 8 of them became litigants who appealed. This category falls between the defeatist response of most litigants who did not appeal and the overtly optimistic response of most litigants who appealed.

The final group of litigants were dissatisfied with their lower court treatment but believed that their treatment would be better in the appellate court. The litigants in this group were the most likely to appeal. These litigants had a very positive attitude toward the appellate court. They focused on positive attributes of the appellate court, which they contrasted with the attributes of the district court. They expected the appellate court to focus on the social issues they considered as the heart of their claim.

These three conceptions of the appellate court are consistent with the two ideal-types of the role of appellate courts — *error correction* and *policy making* — found in the legal literature (e.g., Hart 1941, 1961; Meador 1974).[3] The primary distinction between those litigants who approximated the error-correction ideal-type and those litigants who approximated the policy-making ideal-type, both described below, occurred in their differing expectations of the procedures to be used by the appellate court. The litigants who paralleled the policy-making ideal-type had created a list of attributes that they associated with the appellate court, and these attributes were usually identified as positive by the litigants who appealed. In contrast, those litigants who were closer to the error-correction ideal-type did not conceive of the appellate court as incorporating any different attributes than those they associated with the trial court. Indeed, the *similar court/same outcome* version, to be described below, appears to explain all the litigants who did not appeal but the 4 satisfied ones. Using the coin analogy, even if they thought the coin had two sides, the litigants who did not appeal saw no way in which another flip of the coin *by the same or similar people* would lead to a different result.

The Error-Correction Ideal-Type

The first ideal-type is error correction: appellate action is an attempt to rectify errors created by lower levels in the court system (Dalton 1985, 73–74). Within this ideal-type, the appellate process is considered as a normal part of the judicial procedure; that is, the appellate process is simply another level in the court system that a litigant can encounter. Just as some litigants encounter the move from settlement conference to bench trial, some litigants also move from an inability to resolve their action at the trial court level to the attempt to resolve it at the appellate level. Although the litigants may expect some changes in the context (just as they noted a change in the context between the settlement conference and the trial), these changes will not significantly affect their view of the manner in which the appellate court will resolve their claim.

The error-correction ideal-type is based on the premise that *like cases are treated alike*. When litigants' cases are not treated in the same manner as cases they perceive as similar to their own, they believe that an error has occurred. As in the case of bureaucratic processing, it is only important to establish the similarity in facts with other cases that were treated differently.

Based on these criteria, the error-correction ideal-type should display the following procedural aspects:

The litigant will view the appellate arena as repeating most (if not all) of the procedures of the trial court. The litigants who did not appeal viewed the appellate court as a replication of their original trial court experiences. As previously noted, litigants who appealed identified the appellate court as an arena in which they expected to encounter procedures different from those that they encountered in the trial court. In contrast, litigants who did not appeal made no distinction between the procedures they expected to be used by the appellate court and those used by the trial court.

The litigant will identify no reason to alter a claim in order to enter the appellate process. The alteration of the claim in such cases occurs not in the losing litigants' views of the important issues in their cases, but their belief that these same issues will become the primary issues for the courts. Litigants who did not appeal did not alter their view of the important issues in their cases: as far as they were concerned the trial court had dealt squarely with the issues at hand. For example, in the current case, this litigant could identify no way of changing her claim in order to convince the court to come to a different conclusion:

> We didn't do the job. We knew we didn't. And to be totally honest, I think the judge knew. The judge knows that we did not do the damage. We didn't do the job. But I think because that third party wasn't subpoenaed in court and didn't testify, we lost. I think the judge did his job by law. (Nonappellant 27: a forty- year-old woman involved in a tort case)

In contrast, it was hard to find litigants who appealed who had not altered their claims (see the policy-making ideal-type below). This appears to be a fundamental difference between the litigants who did not appeal and those who did.

The losing litigant will emphasize the facts of the case over the law. Litigants who did not appeal consistently focused on the facts of their case. They responded to a wide variety of questions by consistently referring to the primary facts in their case, and they saw no need to move beyond such facts in considering their case. Such responses could not be said to focus on a primary issue. Rather, the litigants who did not appeal tended to answer questions by constantly restating their fact situation. This response occurred to a variety of questions relating to a variety of topics. In many ways, the law was largely absent from their stories.

Two Versions of the Error-Correction Ideal-Type. Based on the data, there appear to be two antinomic variations of the error-correction ideal-type: the *second-throw-of-the-dice* version and the *similar court/same outcome* version. In the first version, litigants are more likely to appeal, whereas the litigants categorized by the second version are least likely to appeal.

In the second-throw-of-the-dice version, litigants parallel the thinking of the gambler. If their first roll of the dice comes up a loser, maybe a second roll will be luckier. The second chance theory requires that the litigant identify some potential difference in the next level or else she will reject even the possibility of prevailing. One analogy is that in order to win a coin toss, one must first believe not only that the coin has two sides that are different but that it also has a chance of landing on the winning side. The simplest example of this version would be the case of the litigant seeking to use the courts to force the state government to award welfare benefits. After enough chances, the initial error of the government in not awarding welfare benefits may be rectified. The interviews confirm that the majority of appellants involved in unemployment compensation cases paralleled this version.

The second version, similar court/same outcome, is the antithesis of the first. If litigants expect that the procedure to be used is simply a repeat of their current unsatisfactory experience, they would not choose to repeat such an experience, because one normally does not seek to repeat negative experiences unless there are exceptional circumstances. In this version, litigants can see no such exceptional circumstances. Although they identify the error of the court in the resolution of their cases, litigants have no reason to think the judges of the appellate court would resolve their claims in a more satisfactory manner than did their colleagues in the trial court. This second version seems to capture nonappellants' reactions; they did not view the appellate court as offering any hope of a better process and outcome, but instead viewed the appellate court as a replication of their negative experience in the trial court—an experience they did not wish to duplicate.

Which of these two versions litigants adopt is related to their experience with their current case prior to court involvement. Those litigants who have previously experienced administrative review of their current case are most likely to resemble the second-throw-of-the-dice version. Administrative review occurs when decisions of a government agency are reviewed by internal bureaucratic means. In such cases, litigants are usually processed through a series of bureaucratic reviews prior to court involvement. In unemployment compensation cases, litigants usually have prevailed at some lower stage only to have it reversed at a higher bureaucratic level. Such bureaucratic "flip-flopping" in decisions seemed to promote a second-throw-of-the-dice attitude. Indeed, the second-throw-of-the-dice version applied to only 8 of the 95 litigants who appealed, but all 8 were unemployment compensation cases. Appellant 48, a sixty-year-old man involved in an unemployment compensation case, stated, "If you lose, appeal is the only way open. One more step further." In contrast, those litigants whose cases were initially heard in the trial court and who subsequently lost in the trial court were more likely to feel "burned" by their experience and not to wish to repeat it, thus fitting the similar court/same outcome version. Nonappellant 11 summed up this version when he stated, "I feel victimized every time it goes on."

The interviews indicate that the element that explains the difference between the two versions is the presence of optimism; that is, an expectation of encountering some difference in the procedures of the appellate court. The litigants who did not appeal did not believe that *any* difference in procedure would occur in the appellate court, whereas the litigants who appealed recognized the potential to prevail in the courts in the long term even if the process appears similar from one court to the next.

The Policy-Making Ideal-Type

The second ideal-type is policy making: appellate courts are considered primarily for their policy-making function. The appellate courts act to redefine the issues inherent in the case into the primary issues for policy resolution. Greater legal specialization is applied to cases at the appellate level, and the change in legal context is reflected in the increasing social importance and abstraction of the issues argued before the court.

This ideal-type is premised on the assumption that the overt break between the trial level and the appellate level, which is evident in the different legal procedures for appeal, provokes the litigants to view the appellate process as an advanced level of the judicial hierarchy in which they are able to express their claims. The appellate court assesses the litigants' claims from a perspective different from the trial court. This differing approach, in which the appellate court has greater ability to invoke abstract issues that could not be appropriately considered in the context of the trial court, is reflected in the different procedures adopted by the court in the resolution of claims. Litigants acknowledge the differing approach by altering their claims.

In simple terms, the policy-making ideal-type is characterized by the premise that *each case is judged on its merits*. In opposition to the bureaucratic and routinizing notions of the error-correction ideal-type, the policy-making ideal-type is concerned with accentuating the individual and unique differences inherent in each case. Each case is individual in nature, and this individuality is not exposed by any bureaucratic treatment. Therefore, the litigants seek to accentuate the way in which their case is different from other claims and deserves to be treated with special respect.

Based on these criteria, the policy-making ideal-type should display the following procedural aspects:

The litigant recognizes that the appellate court uses a different process from the trial court in approaching the litigant's claim. The litigants who appealed proposed that the appellate court would have a different approach to their claim. They made a clear distinction between the appellate court and the trial court in terms of such factors as legal experience, sensitivity to new issues, objectivity, and distance from local values. They also identified the appellate court as possessing measures that supported the careful consideration of each claim. As was noted in the last chapter, litigants who appealed consistently compared the positive experience they expected to encounter in the appellate court with the negative experience they had encountered in the trial court. In contrast, litigants who did not appeal viewed any distinction between the lower court and the appellate level as irrelevant.

The litigant will alter her claim in the transition to the appellate process. The litigants who appealed clearly altered their claims in relation to the appellate court. Although most litigants who appealed appeared from the start to view their claim as incorporating important social issues, they made a clear distinction between the inability of the trial court to deal with such issues and their expectation that such issues would become the focus at the appellate level. The alteration of the claim in such cases occurred not in the litigants' views of the important issues in their cases, but in their belief that these same issues would become the primary issues for the courts. Although the litigants who appealed may not have changed their views of the most important issues in their cases, they certainly expected that the appellate court, as opposed to the trial court, would be able to focus on the issues that they defined as most important. They believed that the primary issue for them would also become the primary issue for the appellate court. Litigants who appealed generally felt that the primary issue in their case was not among the issues discussed by the trial court or, in a sense, that the trial court missed the point of the case, but litigants who did not appeal only occasionally mentioned such a feeling.

The litigant will emphasize legal issues rather than the facts of the case. Litigants who appealed, except those in unemployment compensation cases, tended to focus on the issues of law, whereas litigants who did not appeal tended to focus on the facts in the case alone. Litigants who appealed were much more likely to implicitly or explicitly challenge the existing law in their stories, whereas litigants who did not appeal were more likely to simply focus on the facts in their cases. Although litigants who appealed described the facts in their cases, and these facts were integral to understanding their actions, they consistently moved beyond the facts to discuss their views of the law in their cases. For example, Appellant 42 (a fifty-one-year-old man involved in a marriage dissolution case) stated, "Decision [of the court of appeals] is based less on issues than on the law. The trial judge did not consider precedents."

The only exception to this rule occurs in the appellants involved in unemployment compensation cases. These appellants were less likely to focus on the law than other litigants who appealed. In this respect, appellants involved in unemployment compensation claims resembled their counterparts who did not appeal. Such litigants highlighted and re-highlighted the facts of their cases during the interviews.

The policy-making ideal-type is based on the difference of the appellate court from the lower court in terms of process, focus, and the ability to deal with social issues. Those litigants who create a conception of the appellate court in which the appeal process allows the consideration of social issues, such as issues of gender roles or fundamental rights, should be most likely to appeal in those instances in which they believe that their claims embody such social issues. The litigants who appealed viewed their claims as embodying important social issues and identified the appellate courts as better able to respond to such issues. In simple terms, the litigants who appealed viewed the bureaucratic nature of the trial court as unsuited to respond procedurally to the important social issues in their cases. In contrast, these litigants viewed the appellate court as procedurally equipped to recognize and effectively respond to such social issues from a legal standpoint. From this evidence, it appears that most appellants parallel the policy-making ideal-type in their conceptions of the role of the appellate court.

Who Initiates Appeals and Why

In this chapter, I demonstrated that it is possible to create a process-based approach, which highlights the most important procedural aspects of the decision to appeal. However, such an approach is relevant only to the extent that it can explain who appeals and why. The process-based approach pro-

TABLE 14

LOSING LITIGANTS BY SATISFACTION
WITH TRIAL COURT PROCESS

Satisfied	Dissatisfied
Satisfied nonappellants	Similar court/same outcome (nonappellants)
	Second-throw-of-the-dice (appellants)
	Policy making (appellants)

poses that litigants are motivated primarily by the desire to be treated fairly in resolving their claims. The interviews demonstrate that this desire for a positive process is important in two places: those who were satisfied with their district court experience and those who expect to be satisfied with their appellate court experience should they appeal. Some litigants did not appeal because they believed that they had been heard fairly in the district court. Thus, the degree of the litigants' satisfaction with the lower court in terms of process determined the difference between those who accepted their loss with finality and those who did not accept their loss (see table 14).

In the current research, only 4 of the 125 interviews involve litigants who could be classified as satisfied. The satisfied litigants found no reason to appeal because, although they failed to prevail, these litigants identified that they have been heard fairly on the issues in their claim. In the case of such litigants, the conception of the appellate court is largely irrelevant. They had achieved what they wanted; that is, to be heard fairly by the district court. These litigants could identify no reason to consider the possibilities offered by the appellate court, because they were satisfied with the resolution of their claim, and consequently all litigants in this category chose not to appeal.

The desire to be heard in a fair manner was also the cornerstone of the second influential element: the litigants' different conceptions of the appellate court. In this sense, expected satisfaction with the appellate court was the second primary distinction between those who appealed and those who did not appeal. Those litigants who were dissatisfied with the procedures of the trial court could be divided into three groups in terms of their conception of the appellate court (see table 15).

The first group contained those litigants who were dissatisfied with the procedures of the lower court but who identified no reason to appeal. They expected the appellate court to duplicate their recent lower court action in a manner that could lead only to the same result. Because this repeat of procedures would lead to both the same outcome and a similar dissatisfaction with

TABLE 15
DISSATISFIED LOSING LITIGANTS BY CONCEPTION
OF THE APPELLATE COURT

Negative Conception of Appellate Court (Nonappellants)	Positive Conception of Appellate Court (Appellants)
Similar court/same outcome	Second-throw-of-the-dice
	Policy making

the procedures, they saw no reason to duplicate their negative experience. In their conception of the appellate court, these litigants who did not appeal paralleled the similar court/same outcome version of the error-correction ideal-type. This latter group of litigants can be contrasted with those litigants who have a slightly more positive conception of the appellate court. These litigants parallel the second-throw-of-the-dice version of the error-correction ideal-type.

The final group of litigants were dissatisfied with their lower court treatment but believed that their treatment would be better in the appellate court. Such litigants focused on the positive attributes of the appellate court, which they contrasted with the attributes of the district court. They expected the appellate court to focus on the social issues they considered to be at the heart of their claim. This final group paralleled the conception of the appellate court proposed by the policy-making ideal-type.

The conception of the appellate court and the perception of the trial court experience are influenced by the nature of the litigant's claim. Those litigants who had experienced a series of decisions in regard to the same case prior to their arrival at the appellate court were much more likely to adopt the position of the second-throw-of-the-dice version of the error-correction ideal-type. The nature of the claim is important because certain types of claims, such as unemployment compensation cases, are more likely to encounter a variety of quasijudicial decision-making procedures prior to the appellate arena. It appears from the interviews that such prior activity creates different perceptions of the litigants' trial court experience and their subsequent conception of the appellate court.

Litigants' expectations as to the validity of the legal arena as a resolver of disputes are important in this scenario for two reasons. First, litigants who did not trust the legal arena to resolve their dispute are very unlikely to subsequently appeal, even if they have the misfortune to be a party to a trial court action. This may explain the willingness of many nonappellants to reject the concept of an appeal while simultaneously considering violence or noncompliance as a method of resolving their dispute. Second, the litigants' original expectations of the court must find a way to be reconciled with their subsequent trial court experience. Litigants appeared to resolve their claim in two conflicting manners that were dependent on their conception of the appellate court. Some litigants identified their trial court experience as negative and proposed, based on their original expectations, that this experience was an aberration that would not be replicated in appellate actions. These were the litigants who appealed. Other litigants identified their trial court experience as negative and proposed that their original expectations had been incorrect and subsequently resolved not to pursue any future action. In this light, litigants who appealed are those litigants whose expectations are least likely to be diminished by their trial court experience.

Putting the Model Together

This model, based on the ideas articulated by the litigants in regard to the decision to appeal, has the ability to distinguish between those who appeal and those who choose not to appeal. To demonstrate this fact, let me now use the four indicators: (1) the litigants' expectations of the validity of the legal arena as a resolver of disputes; (2) the litigants' satisfaction with the trial court experience; (3) the nature of the litigants' claims; and (4) the litigants' conception of the appellate process—and the various elements that compose each of these indicators—to illustrate their ability to explain who appeals and why. Table 16 reveals a rough version of how each of these indicators relate to the individuals' decisions whether to appeal their loss in a civil court.

Litigants' Expectations of the Validity of the Legal Arena

The Decision to Use the Court

By definition, litigants who appealed must have passed some threshold in regard to their acceptance of the court as able to resolve their existing dispute. A person who does not trust the court to resolve her dispute could potentially still be involved in a trial court action as a defendant (although as previously noted, there are many methods for defendants to avoid being drawn into court actions). However, such reluctant actors are unlikely to subsequently use the appellate court. Consequently, litigants who appealed must accept the court as able to resolve their dispute while litigants who did not appeal could be categorized as rejecting the possibility of the court as a means to resolving their dispute.

Learning from the Trial Court Experience
Interestingly enough, litigants who did not appeal can be categorized as those who learn from their trial court experience, whereas their appealing counterparts are likely to maintain their original expectations of the court as able to resolve their dispute. Each litigant has two possible options in regard to categorizing their trial court loss: they can identify the trial court action as an aberration and maintain their original expectation that the court can resolve their dispute; or they can identify the trial court action as representative of court actions in general and consequently alter their original expectations to make them consistent with their actual experience. The former can be said to maintain their original expectations of the court as a resolver of disputes in the face of contrary evidence, while the latter learn from their trial court experience and alter their expectations accordingly.

Legal research (Paese, Lind, and Kanfer 1988, 202; Paese 1986) has noted that those people who have predefined expectations may not alter their expectations in the face of contrary evidence. In the current study, these are the litigants who appealed. Those who learn that their expectations are inconsistent with the reality of their trial court experience are those who do not appeal.

Satisfaction with the Trial Court Experience

Process
Litigants can define their trial court experience as either positive (satisfied) or negative (dissatisfied) in terms of process. Those who are satisfied with their trial court experience in terms of process are unlikely to appeal. Those litigants who are dissatisfied with their trial court experience in terms of process comprise both those litigants who are least likely to appeal and those who are most likely to appeal. The difference between those who appealed and those who did not appears to be determined primarily by differences in the litigants' conceptions of the appellate court.

TABLE 16
WHO APPEALS AND WHY BASED
ON THE PROCESS-BASED APPROACH

Indicators	Aspect	Element	Likely to Appeal	Unlikely to Appeal
1. Litigants' expectations of the court as a resolver of disputes:				
	a. Litigants' decisions to use the court			
		i. View the court positively	X	
		ii. View the court negatively		X
	b. Learning from their trial court experience			
		i. Litigants learn		X
		ii. Litigants do not learn	X	
2. Litigants' satisfaction with their trial court experience:				
	a. Process			
		i. Satisfied		X
		ii. Not satisfied	X	X
3. The nature of the litigant's claim				
	a. The legal system's definition of the claim			
		i. Extensive prior experience	X	
		ii. Limited prior experience	X	X

TABLE 16 (CONTINUED)

	b. The litigant's definition of the claim			
		i. Court failed to deal with "real" issues	X	X
		ii. Court dealt with real issues		X
		iii. Abstract social issues incorporated	X	
		iv. Only routine issue incorporated		X
	c. Audience			
		i. Perceived audience is wide	X	
		ii. Perceived audience is narrow		X
4. Litigants' conception of the appellate court				
	a. Error-correction ideal-type			
		i. Second-throw-of-the-dice version	X	
		ii. Similar court/ same outcome version		X
	b. Policy-making ideal-type	i. Policy-making version	X	

The Nature of the Claim

The Legal System's Definition of the Issues

The legal system's definition of the issues became important in an indirect manner. One would presuppose that the legal definition of a claim is important in itself. However, the interviews indicate that the legal definition was more important instead as an indicator of the likelihood of litigants having previously encountered a series of administrative, quasijudicial, and judicial decisions in regard to their claim. This fact indicates that the nomenclature is incorrect in this respect and that a better definition would come under the category of *prior experience*. Those litigants with extensive prior experience of a variety of decisions (by definition, both negative and positive) in regard to their claim were more likely to appeal. Yet this characteristic is not defining in all cases, because litigants with less prior experience were present as both appellants and nonappellants.

Litigants' Definition of the Issues

The fact that litigants maintain an independent assessment of the salient issues in their claim emerged as important in two ways. First, it was a source of dissatisfaction among many litigants that the trial court had failed to adequately consider the issues as defined by them rather than by the legal system. Second, the manner in which litigants defined the issues in their cases created a distinction between those who were more likely to appeal and those who were less likely to appeal. Litigants who defined their claims as involving abstract social principles (the right to work, gender roles, higher principles, etc.) were more likely to appeal, as opposed to those litigants who simply defined their cases in terms of the narrow resolution of their current limited dispute. Such litigants were more likely to appeal because they were also more likely to identify the appellate court as an arena that was better equipped than the trial court to deal with abstract social issues. In contrast, those litigants who identified their claims as involving "no big issues" were least likely to pursue appellate action. Interestingly, there is no real indication that such distinctions were inherent in the legal definition or categorization of the claims. On another note, this category also seems to incorporate parts of the distinction created in Baum's (1981) theory of who appeals as outlined in chapter 2.

Audience

In the prior category, those litigants who identified their claim as involving wider social principles were also more likely to identify a wider potential audience for the meaning of their claim. Either as a direct correlation with the previous category or possibly independent of it, those litigants who identified their claim as involving a wider audience were more likely to appeal. Those litigants who identified their claim as involving only a narrow audience were least likely to wish to appeal.

Litigants' Conception of the Appeals Court

There appeared to be three different conceptions of the appellate court. Those litigants who expected the appellate court to be different from their trial court experience were the most likely to appeal. Litigants who attributed positive characteristics to the appellate court in regard to the subsequent treatment of their claim were the most likely to appeal. This group was composed of people who thought that the appellate court would incorporate all of those elements whose absence in the trial court were identified by litigants as the source of their subsequent dissatisfaction with their court experience. The litigants who expected such positive attributes in the appellate court were more likely to identify their own cases as involving important social issues, and they expected that such issues would receive better treatment in the appellate arena due to the presence of such positive attributes.

The second category of litigants conceived of the appellate arena as much like the trial court but saw no disadvantage in having a second chance at prevailing. This position was consistent with those litigants who had a great deal of prior experience with administrative, quasijudicial, and judicial decisions in regard to the current case. This group of litigants expected little difference in the attributes of the appellate court but was still very likely to appeal.

The third category expected the appellate court to replicate the trial court in every way, including their negative experience. Since they could conceive of no difference in the appellate court from the trial court, these litigants identified no reason to replicate their negative experience and were the least likely to appeal.

How the Process Relates to the Outcome

The current model assumes that the outcome is defined as a product of the process. Using the analogy of a coin flip, in the current model, the person who flips the coin is identified as determining the possible range of subsequent outcomes. Some litigants identified that the new coin flipper (i.e., the appellate court) would bring the possibility of a different outcome. This perspective can be found in two conceptions of the appellate court—the policy-making ideal-type and the second-throw-of-the-dice version of the error-correction ideal-type. In contrast, some litigants identified the new coin flip (i.e., their expected appellate court experience) as a duplication of the prior coin flip (i.e., their trial court experience), and they assumed that such activity could result only in a replication of the previous outcome. This perspective can be found in the similar court/same outcome version of the error-correction ideal-type. In either case, the process is seen as directly shaping the possible results.

From the perspective of the litigants, outcome cannot be separated from the process used to achieve that outcome. The decision maker is specifically attributed a determinant role in the shape of the final outcome (Thibaut and Walker 1975; Lind and Tyler 1988; Tyler 1990). The potential bias of a legal decision maker is important only to the extent that one thinks that outcome can be shaped by such biases. While it is true that considerations of the biases of legal decision makers will also affect assessments of process, the potential biases of a legal decision maker become determinant only when the outcome is seen as a direct product of the process. For example, I may be despised by the person who flips the coin in a coin flip, but (assuming the use of a properly weighted two-sided coin) it is hard to say that their bias against me would determine the outcome. Therefore, such biases are unlikely to become a major focus of my consideration of the likely outcomes of a coin flip. Instead, I am more likely to focus on my luck or the probability of either side landing face up. However, in the case of legal decision making, the litigants identify that the nature of the process is such that biases on the part of the legal decision maker translate into set outcomes. They begin from the assumption that the coin has a potential to be improperly weighted or one-sided.

In fact, once outcome is no longer identified as a neutrally derived process, one is apt to focus on the process as the major consideration in regard to the decision whether to appeal. From this perspective, consideration of outcome cannot be derived independently of an evaluation of the process to be used to reach that outcome. If a process is biased against you, then you can assume only that you will receive a negative outcome; that is, if you do not receive a fair trial, it is highly unlikely that you would receive a fair outcome.

In the case of the litigants, process determined the outcome in terms of the four possible variations evidenced in regard to the decision to appeal:

> 1. The process was perceived as fair and the outcome was negative such that the litigants felt that any fair court experience could lead

only to a similar outcome. Thus, these litigants were satisfied with the outcome. This accounted for the 4 satisfied nonappellants in the interviews.

2. The process was perceived as unfair and the outcome was negative such that the litigants assumed that any future court experience would also be similarly unfair and consequently would lead to a replication of the negative outcome. Thus, the appellate court would replicate the process of the trial court and this could result only in a similar outcome. This accounted for the similar court/same outcome conception of the appellate court.

3. The process was perceived as unfair and the outcome was negative such that the litigants assumed that any future court action must be fairer and consequently might not lead to a replication of the negative outcome. In fact, the expected attributes and behavior of the appellate court were such that it actually facilitated the handling of the issues in the litigants' claims in a manner that the trial court could not have handled them. This accounted for the policy-making conception of the appellate court.

4. Although the process was perceived as unfair and the outcome was negative, the losing litigants had experienced similar situations in the past only to have them later reversed. The litigants expected the possibility of a positive outcome as long as the appellate court were fair enough that such a possibility was not precluded by any bias on the part of the appellate court. This accounted for the litigants with the second-throw-of-the-dice conception.

In each case, process is identified as directly determining the possible range of outcomes, and the current four variations arise from the different possible conceptions of the potential process that the litigants expected to encounter in the appellate court. Changes in the conceptions of the process are directly correlated with changes in the likely subsequent outcomes. It should be noted that in the case of the litigants who appealed, as presented in the final two categories, the outcome reverts not to a positive outcome but rather becomes the *possibility* of a positive outcome.

Conclusion

Using the ideas laid out in the procedural justice literature, I developed a process-based approach to the decision to appeal. This approach, consistent with the litigants' behavior and their ideas regarding the decision to appeal, has the ability to explain who appeals and why. Such an approach is the antithesis of the outcome-based approach adopted traditionally by legal scholars in considering the decision to appeal.

In the next chapter, I consider the ability of the two approaches to explain a wide range of the activities of individuals in relation to the judiciary, including the issues of compliance, legitimacy, and court-related violence. I argue that the real utility of a process-based approach emerges only when we consider this approach in terms of its practical and theoretical implications.

4.

A New Perspective on Individual Behavior

To date, when legal scholars have considered why individuals appeal, it has been assumed that they do so because they desire a certain goal and that goal can be attained only by achieving a positive outcome in their court case. The logic appears to make sense. If one's goal is to end segregation in schools, it is logical that one would desire to win cases like *Brown* in order to achieve such a goal (see Kluger 1976; Tushnet 1987; Wasby 1995). Similarly, if one's goal is to get a painter to compensate one for a poorly painted house, it is logical that such a goal occurs only if one wins the case. In keeping with this outcome-based approach, it has been assumed that the failure to win such cases should be identified as a rejection of a litigant's claim.

In this chapter, I argue that the process-based approach offers legal scholars a new perspective on why individuals appeal. In developing this new perspective, I extend Zemans's (1983) argument, that legal mobilization occurs through the cumulative effect of individual cases on the courts' policy making, to more explicitly designate the litigants who appeal as political actors. Further, I propose that litigants are appealing to the courts specifically because the courts are policy-making institutions. Thus, I revise the traditional image of litigants from viewing them as merely seeking to win to viewing them as appealing in order to have some input into the policy-making process. Litigants seek this input in a way that ensures that their ideas are considered seriously when a policy maker is reaching an outcome that will subsequently have an impact on them. Such a view of litigants must also alter our perspective on the definitions of policy making itself.

As well as offering an explanation of why people appeal that is more consistent with the behavior of litigants and their ideas about the decision whether to appeal, the process-based approach offers insight into compliance and court-related violence, as well as our understanding of the source of the legitimacy of the judiciary. In fact, I posit that it is the traditional focus on the outcome-based approach that has restricted the ability of legal scholars to offer a comprehensive understanding of such issues.

Appealing in Order to Have Policy Input

The outcome-based approach assumes that achieving a successful outcome is the prime motivation that parties have for litigating. It is only upon prevailing that parties are able to implement their desired policy goals (e.g., Rosenberg 1991) or use the legitimacy accorded to legal rights to *begin* the political process of achieving their desired policy goals (e.g., Scheingold 1974). Accordingly, the failure to achieve a positive outcome is synonymous with a failure in general legal terms. The prior litigation is defined as a waste of time, as it is assumed that the inability to win a case becomes synonymous with a lack of change in the positions of the parties. To return to our earlier examples; if Thurgood Marshall and the Legal Defense Fund of the NAACP had failed to "win" the *Brown* case, it would have been considered a waste of resources to have engaged in the case at all because African American children still could not attend integrated schools. Similarly, if someone fails to win his case against the person who shoddily painted his house, the house is destined to remain in that state.

Success in this approach is defined as receiving a judgment that is directly determined by your preferred goal. A party thinks that the outcome should look like A, where A is a series of parameters designed to define the desired policy (cf. Kritzer 1991). Therefore, a party, usually through his lawyer, makes legal rationalizations to the courts for viewing the policy implications in his case in terms of A. He is successful if the decision of the court closely correlates with A, such that the party has made a successful policy claim only when the court's decision looks like A.

Such an approach relies on a zero-sum notion — one either wins or loses — and the loss of a case is defined as both a rejection of the claim and a rejection of the litigant's arguments. According to the outcome-based approach, the failure to achieve a positive outcome is synonymous with a failure in general terms, and the prior activity is defined as a waste of time, as it is assumed that the inability to win a case becomes synonymous with a lack of change in the positions of the parties.

Notwithstanding the difficulty of defining every case in simple win/ lose scenarios when both parties may not receive exactly what they desire from the outcome (Kritzer 1991), the real problem with such an approach is that it fails to account for any effect that the involvement in the actual process produces in the parties. While legal scholars have adopted the outcome-based approach with its focus on winning and losing, they have simultaneously acknowledged that involvement in the process has meaning for the actors, independent of the subsequent outcome. For example, the fact that the United States Supreme Court chose to hear the *Brown* case is considered important in itself, both in terms of the role of the NAACP and in terms of the signal that it sends to African Americans about their future ability to access the political system (see Kluger 1976; Tushnet 1987; Wasby 1995). Similarly, it is considered meaningful by legal scholars that disputes are resolved in a setting with a fair process (e.g., Harrington 1985) rather than through alternatives that guarantee a positive outcome but appear questionable in terms of procedural fairness (e.g., Merry 1979, 1990).

Such a finding should not be surprising, considering the fact that individuals participate in a great many interactions in which scholars define the very act of participation as important, independent of the subsequent outcomes. The widespread participation by individuals in elections is but one of the most obvious examples of such activity. The act of participation is important in such a context, because the subsequent outcome is achieved by a process that involves each of the subsequently affected parties. The value of such participation is assumed traditionally to lie in the ability to have one's ideas heard and considered in a fair manner in reaching a conclusion — the very basis of the process-based approach.

Such a proposition complements the role that Pitkin (1967; see also Gosnell 1969) offers for government institutions in a representative government. Pitkin states that

> representative government requires that there be machinery for the expression of the wishes of the represented, and that the government responds to these wishes unless there are good reasons to the contrary. *There need not be a constant activity of responding, but there must be a constant condition of responsiveness, of potential readiness to respond.* It is not that a government represents only when it is acting in response to an express popular wish; a representative government is one that is responsive to popular wishes when there are some. *Hence there must be institutional arrangements for*

responsiveness to these wishes. Again it is incompatible with the idea of representation for the government to frustrate or resist the people's will without good reason, to frustrate or resist it systematically or over a long period of time. *We can conceive of the people "acting through" the government even if most of the time they are unaware of what it is doing, so long as we feel that they could initiate action if they so desired* [emphasis added]. (Pp. 232–33)

Using the framework proposed by Pitkin, the ability to appeal can be defined as an *institutional arrangement for responsiveness* in relation to the population within a set jurisdiction. The appellate court offers people the opportunity to alter the policy articulated by the lower courts. The judiciary has institutionalized an arrangement whereby it can systematically offer a point of access to litigants in order to maintain the possibility of *responsiveness.* Within such a framework, the importance of the appellate court as a political institution lies in the ability of people to *initiate* appeals that have the potential to alter the existing policy. This contrasts with the ability to use the appellate court to successfully alter policy in every case. The appellate court is providing a point of access to which dissatisfied litigants (or citizens) can press their claims for change in the existing policy. The ability to initiate appeals fulfills the requisite action of responsiveness independent of the successful completion of policy change.

To this effect, Zemans (1983) has argued that individuals who use the courts are involved in an act of political participation. She proposed that the cumulative effect of each individual's decision to use the courts corresponds to a legal mobilization, such that "in the simplest case, a particular behavior is demanded by verbal appeal to the law. The law is thus mobilized when a desire or want is translated into a demand as an assertion of one's rights. At the same time that the legitimacy of one's claim is grounded in rules of law, the demand contains an implicit threat to use the power of the state on one's own behalf" (Zemans 1983, 700). Yet Zemans was purposely unclear about whether individuals identified such activity in terms of political participation. Instead, in her examples, she sited the locus of political participation as occurring in the very act of the court's response to the cumulative effect of such demands.

Other scholars have been less reticent on this issue. For example, Lawrence (1991b, 464–65) speculated that "litigation, at all levels, may fulfill the purposes of democracy as set out in classical democratic theory better than the forms of political participation focused on in modern democratic theory, not by protecting unalienable rights, although of course the courts have done that, but by providing litigants with opportunities to participate actively in decisions that significantly affect them." Lawrence identifies the act of litigating as political participation, and she shifts the locus of political participation to the individual. Thus, individuals become political actors who "are engaging in a dialogue about the proper relationship between public and private goods, although we may not speak explicitly in those terms" (Lawrence 1991b, 469).

The nature of the process-based approach leads me to define the litigants as political actors. However, unlike Lawrence, who compares the active act of initiating litigation with the passive act of voting, I am going to propose that the process-based approach is more consistent with viewing the litigants in terms of lobbyists or protesters. A lobbyist within the halls of the legislature is challenging the legislature to alter its existing policy on an issue. Similarly, protesters are directly attributed with challenging the government to change its articulated policy on a set issue. In each case, the individual is challenging the government to alter its articulated policy. The individual is expressing his opinion to an agency of government in the hope that the targeted policy-making institution will consider his ideas in the creation of future policy on a specific matter.

In the same fashion, an appellant explicitly or implicitly challenges the decision of the lower court through the initiation of an appeal. Yet the lower court is articulating the current policy of the state. Thus, each appellant is challenging the appellate court to alter the state's policy in order to gain a more favorable outcome. Even if the litigant thinks that the court has simply made an error in articulating the existing law, he is still challenging the articulated policy of the state. The lower court decision determines the very shape of government policy as it applies to the litigant, and this decision represents the articulation of that policy in relation to the litigant. Whether correct or not from the point of view of the litigant, such policy has state sanction and therefore represents state policy. Until such time as the trial court decision is altered (for example, by appellate review or by legislation), the trial court decision remains the articulation of state policy of the relevant issue. In some cases, the litigant's challenge to state policy is obvious, but the challenge exists in all cases because the cumulative impact of even relatively insignificant changes can drastically alter policy over time (see Lindblom and Braybrooke 1963; Zemans 1983).

Policy change may appear to be the direct motivation of litigants involved in "political" cases, such as civil rights or civil liberties. However, the "ordinary" litigant seeking a divorce, or monetary compensation for a breached contract or personal injury, has been painted as self-interested and less socially motivated than his "political" counterparts in the courts or in other arenas of government.[1] This proposition is incorrect from both a theoretical and a practical standpoint. From a theoretical standpoint, it can be argued that the litigant is motivated by his self-interest to the same degree as his political counterparts. In fact, some theorists, such as Downs (1957) and Olson (1965), assume that self-interest is the primary motivation of *all* political actors. For example, does Linda Brown, as a black child in a segregated society, have any less self-interest in the outcome of her case than a woman seeking to terminate her previous marriage? From a practical standpoint, the interviews clearly demonstrate that most litigants who appeal identify their claims in terms of altering precedent or principle. The appellants present issues to the judiciary that they believe have wide-ranging social consequences, and they appeal in order to invoke the power of the courts to have an impact on such social issues. Therefore, it appears that it is more appropriate to identify litigants who appeal as political actors.

The image of the litigants that I am developing extends the original theory offered by Zemans (1983) by defining the litigants as political actors who are aware of the implications of their actions. The litigants are political actors because they have mobilized their resources in an effort to force the government, in the form of the judiciary, to intervene on their behalf (Zemans 1983; Lawrence 1991a, 1991b). By continuing in the court system, they are articulating the manner in which they would like to have their conflict resolved. By refusing to accept the initial decision of the government (in the form of the opinion of the trial court), the appellants establish an interactive process between themselves and the government (in the form of the judiciary) in which they directly question the decision of a government agency (in the form of the trial court). They seek to alter (by appealing for a different decision) the articulated policy of the government (in the form of the trial court decision). In this sense, the appellants are most like their lobbyist counterparts in the halls of the legislature or their protesting counterparts in the streets. They are attempting policy change through an ongoing "dialogue" with a policy-making institution—a definition originally used by Lawrence (1991b, 469).

The following statement by Appellant 71, which was already noted in chapter 2, sums up this idea from the litigants' perspective:

> I would like to be able to write that down and offer it to [the court of appeals] as a view from my perspective of what I need or what I see. I . . . I don't know whether I would need to speak directly to them. I . . . I . . . I might . . . I might want to . . . to put myself in that position of actually vulnerability, because I have no idea. I mean, they'd probably scare me to death. But if they were genuinely interested in what the right thing is to do, then they would solicit my input and my perspective and incorporate it into their array of information. I wouldn't necessarily ask them to . . . I mean, I . . . I . . . it would satisfy me if they sought that kind of input with open minds and right-heart attitudes. And I wouldn't hold them to ruling a particular way if I felt like they were genuinely listening and genuinely concerned. And I think that's still possible within the legal system, but sometimes you don't see it.

The very act of litigating carries meaning in itself for the litigant, and it appears to work in several ways. First, it validates the original complaint of the litigant by having its value confirmed by the fact that the court takes it seriously. Simultaneously, the fact that the court takes the litigant's ideas seriously in considering a result is taken as evidence that the litigant has effectively exposed the wrongdoing of the other party in a public arena. Thus, it is the very nature of the court's process that is important in meeting the litigants' goals. Further, it is only in the court where such goals can be met.

For example, in the previous statement, Appellant 71 speaks directly of what the judges should be concerned about as judges; she wants the *court* to be "genuinely listening and genuinely concerned." This point is crucial because it is the *court* that is important in meeting these goals. In contrast, any third party that expressed interest in her claim and appeared to be "genuinely listening and genuinely concerned" would presumably not meet these criteria; for example, her friends' interest in her claim is not sufficient to meet her goal for the litigation. Instead, her focus is on the court itself as the institution that can fulfill these criteria and meet her goals. It is the authority accorded to the court that is important in the current interviews in allowing the litigants to think that their involvement in the process is sufficient to meet their goals. In such an approach, the power of the court arises from the fact that the court offers an arena in which dissatisfied parties can have their claims accorded an equal status with the existing policy. The nature of the court's procedures are such that the litigants' ideas are treated as a credible alternative to the existing policy, at least for the duration of the litigation. And it is important in such a context that it is an authoritative and public institution, such as the court, where the litigants are able to articulate their claims. The parties are accorded status simply because the court's procedures publicly treat their claims as equal and credible alternatives to the existing policy.

As noted in chapter 2, the court experience was identified as punishing the other party by exposing his wrongdoing or hypocrisy in a public forum. This exposure of the other party occurs, according to the litigant's perspective, because, by treating it as equal and credible, the court has retroactively validated the original claim of the litigating party as always having been worthy of being taken seriously. This is an especially powerful message in cases in which the litigants feel that their claim has previously been belittled or disregarded by the other party; or, as the current interviews show, in which the litigants feel that the behavior of the lower court has denigrated their claim. The other party receives the message, merely from the process of the court and the act of litigating, that he was wrong in not taking the litigant's claim seriously when it was first raised.

The process-based approach offers some insight into this interaction. We can see from the interviews that the courts are not passive actors in this "dialogue." Their prior opinions tenuously shape the litigants' cultural perceptions of the effectiveness of using the judicial arena. Such activity occurs on a cultural level in the way that the litigants view the ability of the courts to resolve their conflicts prior to entering the judicial system. The litigants who appealed clearly identified the appellate courts in terms of their level of support for the goals of many social groups, from women to single parents. This interaction also occurs on an individual level. As Sarat and Grossman (1975, 1202) noted, "the very structure of a dispute-resolving institution may have important influence on the way the dispute is presented; indeed it may affect the basic nature of the dispute itself." The interviews demonstrate that there is a link between the articulated behavior of the court and the expected behavior of the court on some specific issues. For example, the litigants were strongly influenced by their perceptions of the district court, and such perceptions defined their subsequent conception of the appellate court.

Like voters weighing the promises of a party before voting, litigants weigh the attitude of the appellate court toward them before entrusting the resolution of their dispute to the court. In weighing the attitude of the courts toward them, the litigants consider the treatment of similarly situated litigants in order to determine the courts' position in regard to them as a representative of a social group. Thus, a woman may look to historically positive court decisions involving the rights of women and determine that courts in general are supportive of her as a woman challenging the terms of her marriage dissolution. The courts' history shapes the litigant's expectations of the courts, including her expectations of her chance to have an impact on the creation of policy by the appellate court.

The difference proposed by the process-based approach is that the litigants weigh the courts' attitude toward them based on the courts' treatment of similar litigants rather than simply basing such an analysis on the prior success, or lack of it, of similar litigants. In this context, participation in the process counts for something of value to the potential litigants. For example, the fact that the courts considered the arguments of women in prior cases and treated these arguments seriously in their determination of a final decision is an important signal to women independent of the outcome of the case. In such an approach, it is the fact that the court offers a point of access for the litigants to the policy-making arena that becomes important, rather than the subsequent outcome. From this perspective, the litigants are interested in the ability to have input into the final decision in a manner that allows the litigants' ideas to influence *but not determine* the final outcome. The process-based approach attributes the legal decision maker with the ability to determine the nature of the final outcome, and the litigants focus on this ability because they are interested in ensuring that their ideas and arguments are considered as part of the process of determining the final outcome. Such a perspective does not begin from the assumption that a successful outcome is defined as directly correlated with the litigant's definition of a successful outcome, when both the litigant and the court agree on *A*. Instead, the litigant presents a series of arguments or a way of approaching the issues under consideration, for example *A*, which he wishes the court to consider as part of its final decision. With the process-based approach, the litigant would be satisfied with the outcome even if the outcome were something different, say *B,* as long as his arguments have been heard and considered in a fair manner. Being heard and considered in a fair manner is defined as ensuring that the arguments are considered as part of arriving at the final decision such that the final decision incorporates appropriately all of the possible arguments in developing the resultant outcome.

The process-based approach rests on the premise that individuals appeal because they want their ideas to be heard and considered in a fair manner. But based on this extension of Zemans's notion of legal mobilization, we can append a corollary statement to this original proposition: individuals appeal to the appellate courts specifically because the appellate courts act to create and articulate the policies of the government. As Lawrence (1991a, 467; see also 1991b) argued, "litigation is an important form of self-government in that it allows the individual to invoke the power of the state on his own behalf." Courts create policies through case law and statutory interpretation of existing law. They articulate this law through the publication of opinions and the systematic power of precedent on the resolution of future cases. Decisions have the potential to extrapolate each individual claim to incorporate all similarly situated present and future parties within a defined region. Although most cases are heard at the lowest end of the judiciary's pyramid of power, the appellate decisions, which represent the middle and upper echelons of the pyramid, exercise the greatest political influence over the widest number of people. The decision of an appellate court directly affects the outcome of similar claims by determining the policy of the government toward the acceptable resolution of such cases within the same jurisdiction. In such a context, the appellate courts are directly defining the policy of the state on the relevant issue. For example, the judiciary has created and articulated comprehensive policies on a range of issues from the dissolution of marriages to the relationship of governments with indigenous populations.

This perspective offers us a way to understand the decision to appeal as an act designed not merely to achieve a desired outcome but instead as an act designed to compel an institution of the state to consider the input of the individual in its subsequent formulation of state policy. In other words, litigants enter the courts in order to have their ideas heard by policy makers with the possibility that such ideas are subsequently incorporated into the final policy articulated by the court. From such a position, the focus on process is not simply a means of ensuring that the process is not biased against one in a manner that precludes the possibility of a positive outcome. Instead, the focus on process occurs because the litigants want to be taken seriously and treated fairly in regard to the issues in their claims. Such a hope can be considered independently of the final outcome.

This desire to be heard in a fair manner may explain the anomaly of the Palestinians appealing to the Israeli High Court of Justice despite the completely overwhelming rejection rate in terms of outcome. As noted by Shamir (1991), the Israeli High Court of Justice places Palestinian litigants who appeal in what (until the start of the talks with the PLO as part of the Oslo Peace Accord) has been the only arena in which Palestinians could express complaints to the Israeli civilian government, which was charged with overseeing the Israeli military forces in the Occupied Territories. The Israeli High Court of Justice offered an opportunity to Palestinians in the West Bank and the Gaza Strip to have their complaints treated with some seriousness; as denoted simply by, if nothing else, the time spent by the High Court in hearing such complaints in a system that has otherwise structurally ignored the complaints of such Palestinians.

Similarly, such a logic may also lie at the heart of the increasing use of the courts by African Americans into the 1940s (Kluger 1976; Tushnet 1987; Marable 1991). The federal courts represented the only major policy-making avenue open to African Americans during this period (Weiss 1983; Marable 1991). Notwithstanding the limited success of such appeals by African Americans in terms of outcome, the fact that the court heard such appeals may have acted to satisfy some of the reasons African Americans had for appealing. The United States Supreme Court was the only policy-making institution that appeared willing to listen to the arguments of African Americans in regard to the issue of segregation. Although the Supreme Court offered only limited solace for African Americans in this period,[2] the fact that there was one policy-making institution willing to hear and consider these arguments may have acted to discourage such African Americans from seeking nonsystemic alternatives (Marable 1991; Tushnet 1987). This logic may also explain the fact that the Brown decision is considered such a turning point in African American politics (e.g., Carmichael and Hamilton 1967; Cleaver 1968), despite the fact that the outcome led to virtually no major change in compliance for nearly fourteen years (Giles and Gatlin 1980; Rosenberg 1991).

In simple terms, the importance of the appellate courts lies in their ability to allow litigants to have an impact on the nature of future policy. The litigants who appealed expressed an expectation of greater satisfaction with the appellate court because it would allow them to present their challenge to the existing policy. Although the appellate court might not subsequently alter the policy in their favor, which was openly acknowledged by the low expectation of prevailing by most litigants who appealed, the appellate court would respond to their current political challenge to the existing policy by incorporating their argument into the policy-making process. In this sense, the litigants who appealed were seeking a resolution of their conflict in a manner that satisfied them that their complaint about the existing policy was given credence by the appellate court as a political institution.

This role, the appellate court as a point of access, fits with earlier findings on the legitimating aspects of appellate courts in relation to political regimes. Shapiro (1980) and Dalton (1985) argued that the right to appeal is fundamental to all political regimes because it is required to maintain the legitimacy of the current political system. They maintained that such arrangements are essential not only to representative governments but to all stable political regimes. Shapiro (1980, 635) proposed that government leaders use appeal as a form of patronage to maintain systemic legitimacy: "appeal all the way to the top, and intervention at the top that is perceived as benevolent to the successful appellant, are powerful means of fostering loyalty to the central regime." In this context, appealing is identified as a political act involving the machinery of government in an attempt to be responsive to the demands of the individual.

This perspective challenges the traditional orthodoxy of law that proposes that a court decision has an impact on the relevant parties (and potential parties) such that one expects a change in the general behavior of the society in order to comply with the court's interpretation of the law. In such a context, the law matters because it leads to a change in behavior. Legal scholars have been quick in challenging this orthodoxy by pointing out that most court decisions do not apparently lead to general changes in behavior (e.g., Muir 1967; Scheingold 1974; Rosenberg 1991; McCann 1994). Yet, in doing so, these same scholars have largely reduced the debate of the policy effects of court decisions to a series of methodological questions — where and how to determine *if* a court decision has had an impact on the society (e.g., Simon 1992; Feeley 1992; McCann 1992, 1996; Rosenberg 1996). Legal scholars have consequently argued about the impact (or lack of it) apparent in regard to various court decisions and whether these findings (either pro or con) are methodologically valid (e.g., Wasby 1970; Becker and Feeley 1973; Giles and Gatlin 1980; Johnson and Canon 1984; Songer and Sheehan 1989). To date, scholars on both sides of this methodological debate have assumed that the courts can be defined as policy makers only in those contexts in which court decisions can be found to have had an impact, in the shape of a subsequent change in behavior, on society's members. Thus, they have never truly confronted the possibility that even if a decision of a court is greeted with massive noncompliance and appears to have no impact in terms of a subsequent change in behavior by society's members, the decision could still have important policy consequences.

I propose that scholars, such as Rosenberg (1991) and McCann (1994), may be mistaken in searching for the impact of court decisions only in terms of subsequent compliance. The process-based approach lends credibility to the notion that the impact of court decisions may occur more in the message that is sent to the affected groups about their ability to access the political system than in the resultant change in behavior that accompanies a positive court outcome (e.g., Stalans and Kinsey 1994). In this context, the real impact of *Brown* and *Roe* might lie in the courts' message that African Americans and women, respectively, did not need to seek alternatives outside of the political system in order to have their ideas heard because there was still at least one avenue open to the policy-making arena—the courts. *Brown* would be important, independent of the amount of subsequent desegregation over the next fourteen years and the amount of times that the specific case was referred to by black leaders (cf. Rosenberg 1991), because the role of the case would simply be to signal that the political system was willing to hear the political demands proffered by African Americans. Similarly, despite its overwhelming rejection rate of their demands, the importance of the decision by the Israeli High Court of Justice to continue to hear Palestinian cases is that it demonstrated that the High Court represented the only real avenue open in the Israeli political system (until the recent changes) for Palestinians in the West Bank and Gaza Strip to have an input into Israel's policy on the Occupied Territories.

In such a context, it is possible that the courts can be policy makers even if there is no subsequent change in the behavior of the general society. If we take a process-based approach to litigation and grant the possibility that some parties litigate in order to have input into the policy-making process in the hope of influencing the final decision, it is possible to view the courts as policy makers even if the subsequent policy is unlikely to create a change in the behavior of the general society. The court plays an important role by offering a point of access to the policy-making arena, and parties litigate in order to be heard fairly as part of the process by which a final policy is developed. It is this function that assures parties that their ideas are valued by the government in creating policy, even if the subsequent policy does not correlate with the parties' desired policy wishes. Such a function for the courts is also present even if the courts are unable to make good on many of their policy-making decisions. In such a context, it is the expressive behavior of policy input that becomes important rather than the eventual ability to transform the behavior of the general society in a way that comports with the parties' policy wishes.

Overall, according to the perspective that I am proposing, appealing can be identified as individuals seeking to have input into the decision making in regard to policies that affect them. The importance of the appellate court lies in the fact that the court offers a point of access for individuals to the policy-making arena, and it offers a structured means for individuals to have their ideas considered by those who have the ability to make the final policy regarding them. This approach directly contrasts with the zero-sum logic attributed to most litigants. The traditional explanations are based on the assumption that "everyone prefers winning to losing and winning big to winning small" (Posner 1985, 8). In the current case, winning and losing becomes less important than the ability to have one's say. From this perspective, the logic of appeal relies on the fact that the appeal offers an avenue for voicing one's ideas to an authority who will treat such ideas seriously. In this sense, litigants appeal in order to have a consultative role in shaping the final policy that the courts create. Winning big or winning small become less important than being heard or being heard fairly.

Winners and Losers

The outcome-based approach is based on the premise that litigants are motivated by the desire to win. Such a perspective identifies the parties in any action as being divided into two categories: winners and losers.[3] In this section, I argue that the outcome-based approach's categorization of winners and losers fails to theoretically incorporate aspects of the court experience that are important in explaining the behavior of individuals in the judicial arena.

The problem with such an approach is that the court as an entity is absent. As was noted previously in the book, the outcome-based approach identifies the process — in this case, the decision making undertaken by the court — as a neutral element in the determination of outcome. This limits the ability of the traditional approach to incorporate the facets of the court experience that are important in relation to compliance, legitimacy, and court-related violence. Under the outcome-based approach, if we identify that the losing party is dissatisfied with the outcome, it would be possible to extrapolate from this point to propose that any dissatisfaction the losing party feels about the decision must be directed toward the competing party. In simple terms, if the losing party is unhappy about his loss, he must identify the other party as the source of that unhappiness. Such a logic flows from the fact that the two parties are traditionally identified as adversarial even prior to this loss (Fuller 1981; Felstiner, Abel, and Sarat 1980–81) and the fact that, with the current approach, the gains of the winning party in terms of outcome must be achieved at the expense of the losing party. This unhappiness may, in the case of plaintiffs or no-fault litigants, be in addition to a preexisting feeling of hostility toward the other party for the original injury (Felstiner, Abel and Sarat 1980–1981; Galanter 1983). Overall, the dissatisfaction of the losing litigant appears a wholly fertile source for action in some form against the winning party, as a response to the unhappiness that he is accused of causing.

It is argued traditionally that this unhappiness with the result is the source of the notion of the potential initiator. At the end of every court action, one party always loses in terms of outcome. According to the outcome-based approach, this losing party would prefer to win. Hence, one party is always dissatisfied with the outcome, and this party should, according to this approach, manifest the desire to appeal in order to rectify this loss. In cases in which the ability to appeal is blocked by legal or financial barriers, it is assumed that the litigants are discouraged by such barriers from appealing, but this approach never offers any logic for how litigants proceed to fulfill their desire to win in such cases. It is usually assumed that the realization that their goal cannot be achieved through the courts also removes their motivation to pursue the action in the first place. However, it is possible that the creation of legal or financial barriers to winning in the courts simply encourages litigants to use other arenas in order to resolve their disputes. Consequently, Posner (1985, 6) recognizes that legal and financial barriers should be constructed in a manner that encourages the use of alternative arenas without simultaneously promoting the use of antisystemic methods as a means for individuals to resolve their disputes. The assumption is that even if litigants are precluded from appealing, they will still attempt to find a method to resolve their disputes, independently of the legal system. Notwithstanding Posner's hope to avoid antisystemic alternatives as a method for resolving such disputes, it would appear that the result of this thwarted desire to win is increased noncompliance or violence directed toward the other party as a means of retribution for the loss.

Scholars using the outcome-based approach have considered the issues of compliance (e.g., McEwen and Maiman 1986; Gibson 1989; Casey and Scholz 1991; McGraw and Scholz 1991; Long and Swingen 1991; Gibson 1991; cf. McEwen and Maiman 1984; Morrow 1993) and violence (e.g., Merry 1979) as related directly to the litigants' desire to win. For example, Van Koppen and Malsch (1991) have proposed that many civil litigants, despite their earlier losses in terms of outcome, do in fact "win" by their subsequent acts of noncompliance. As mentioned previously, many litigants demonstrated instances of noncompliance, including moving to other states to avoid fulfilling court judgments. Many other litigants discussed the possibility of simply filing for bankruptcy if their court action were unsuccessful in order to avoid paying the opposing party. These litigants seemed to take pride in their ability to not comply with the trial court's decision, and they felt that their actions adequately punished the other party.

Similarly, the current interviews included some statements of violence directed toward the opposing parties. Merry (1979) proposed that violence was often a ready alternative to court resolution of disputes. A minority of subjects referred to this option in their discussions about alternatives to appealing. As was mentioned briefly in the last chapter, one litigant discussed the possibility that murdering his wife could become the only alternative to appealing (Appellant 68), and several others openly discussed such an option. For example:

> I was reading a *Ladies Home Journal* magazine, and I thought of you when I read this, um, simply because I knew we were gonna be talking about this kind of thing, and this was about a woman who . . . is this appropriate to . . . to mention? [Interviewer: Sure.] Okay [laughter]. Um, it was an article about . . . about, um, the story behind a story, and this was actually a women who was . . . had been five years in, um, a divorce battle, and she ended up committing murder, um, and it says: "Betty's bitterness came to a head in 1989 when she shot Dan Broderick, 44 years old, and his second wife, 28, as they lay asleep in their bed. The killings were preceded by a bitter five-year legal battle over Dan and Betty's possessions and custody of the four kids. It was that conflict, Betty says, that led her to kill her husband, not the fact that he left her for someone else. 'The public has never understood my case at all,' she says. 'He beat the living hell out of me in court. What happened to me was wrong, unjust.'" And I thought, hmm, I . . . I think that that's . . . well, probably that doesn't need any

comment, but, uh, it's one thing to deal with the emotional trauma of a breakup, um, for no apparent reason or a breakup because someone else is involved, but to add insult to injury by being treated unjustly in the court system. (Appellant 71)

Uh, we took them in and explained to them what was going on, and he said, it . . . you know, it's from the stress. And, um . . . and in the anger and the stress, my son will clench his fists [inaudible] body will strain. He's so angry and mad, and one day he came home and said, um, "I'm just . . . I'm gonna put my mom down." I said, "What do you mean by that?" "I'm gonna hurt her. I'm gonna kill her." I said, you know, "It's okay to get mad or it's okay to get angry, but you've got to express it in the right way." (Appellant 37)

The trouble with the outcome-based approach in regard to the implications and consequences of dissatisfaction is that, according to this model, such dissatisfaction should be directed *only* toward the other party and should not involve the court or legal system. As previously noted, the court is identified by the outcome-based approach as a neutral decision maker (like the coin flipper) and consequently cannot be attributed any subsequent blame for the outcome, since the court is identified as removed from any substantial responsibility for the shape of the final outcome. Instead, the outcome is seen as determined by the shape of the proposals of the two competing parties, and the court is identified as simply selecting, using suitable criteria such as prior legal decisions, from these two choices. In this scenario, the court is attributed only limited control over the outcome. Therefore, under the outcome-based approach, any hostility *must* be directed toward the other party.

Yet we know that on many occasions, blame for the ultimate decision is attributed to the presiding judge or the court personnel rather than the opposing party. Further, the litigants' subsequent dissatisfaction about the court's decision is directed toward these entities rather than the opposing party. This dissatisfaction manifests itself in increasing violence directed toward the judges or court personnel for their role in the loss. Virtually every civil court has experienced some example of such violence toward the court personnel (e.g., Johnson and Yerawadekar 1981). Increasingly, trial courts consider the handling of certain civil cases, such as marriage dissolutions, as fraught with the risk of violence against judges and other court personnel (e.g., Johnson and Yerawadekar 1981; Fox 1987; Stevens 1988; Brooks 1989; Geiger 1989; Adams 1990; Gallet 1990; Blau 1992; Cheever and Naiman 1992; Slider 1992; Wax 1992; Hardenbergh 1993). The outcome-based approach is at a loss to explain such incidents against the courts.

Similarly, compliance seems to be directly related to individuals' feelings about their court experience rather than simply their feelings toward the opposing party. Research demonstrates that the greater the level of satisfaction with the process of the courts, the more likely it is that the litigants will subsequently comply with the decisions of the court (McEwen and Maiman 1984; Tyler 1990; Tyler and Rasinski 1991; Wemmers 1995). Unlike what the outcome-based approach would postulate, these studies indicate that dissatisfaction is not simply directed toward the opposing party, and the court is very much a part of the consideration in regard to the implications and consequences of such litigant dissatisfaction.

Moving Away from Winners and Losers

Unlike the outcome-based approach, the process-based approach offers the ability to understand why litigants' dissatisfaction might also be directed toward the courts. According to the process-based approach, the court itself is very much in the litigants' focus in terms of their levels of satisfaction with the subsequent resolution of their dispute. Litigants focused on more than winning and losing; they focused on the procedures that the court used to arrive at that outcome. Consequently, when they were dissatisfied, their dissatisfaction was directed toward the procedures that the court used in deciding their cases. This dissatisfaction occurred in addition to whatever hostility they might feel toward the other party in regard to the original dispute. Such an approach can offer a new perspective on the issues of compliance and court-related violence.

To date, studies (McEwen and Maiman 1984; Tyler 1990; Wemmers 1995) have focused on the notion that losing litigants were more likely to comply if they thought the process was fair. The current approach has the advantage of offering a logic for such an occurrence. Under the current approach, those who are satisfied accept their loss. They accept it not as a defeat or with reluctance, since both categories would lead to dissatisfaction. Instead, they embrace the outcome. To these litigants, the fairness of the court process mitigates their expected unhappiness with the outcome. This occurs because, even though the court decides against them on outcome, the court reached such a decision only after due consideration of both sides of the story. The losing litigants believe that this has ensured that the court has reached a fair (and consequently acceptable) outcome. The fair treatment leads these losing litigants to embrace the decision that leads to greater compliance. Like the distinction between force and authority, the fact that the litigants embrace the decision leads to greater compliance than would occur if they simply felt obliged to fulfill the conditions imposed by a court that they identified as having reached such a decision unfairly.

According to this new perspective, noncompliance represents a rejection of the process used to reach the outcome in the litigants' cases. The litigants demonstrate their belief that the process was unfair by failing to comply with the decisions of the court. Noncompliance occurs because of the actions of the court rather than because of the actions of the other party. We can think of many cases in which we withdraw from compliance because we believe that the process used to reach a decision is patently unfair. For example, we might not comply with the rules promulgated by a newly selected leader, if we believe that his means of attaining the position were not fair. Similarly, one is unlikely to comply with the decisions of a legal institution that he believes has not used a fair method in reaching a decision in his case.

The process-based approach may also explain why judges have increasingly become the target of court-related violence involving "ordinary" civil cases, such as marriage dissolutions. As the interviews note, dissatisfaction among most litigants remained focused squarely on the procedures of the court. Consequently, blame was attributed to the court rather than to the opposing party. Under such considerations, it is not surprising that violence, which is related to the litigants' level of dissatisfaction with their court experience, is therefore also directed toward the judge. Losing parties blame the court because they feel that the court is responsible in that it has used an unfair process in considering their case. According to the dissatisfied litigants, the court has failed to offer them a means through which their claim could be heard in a fair manner and considered as part of reaching a final decision.

Under the process-based approach, the blameworthiness of the judge is compounded by the fact that the decision maker (or judge) was directly attributed a determining role in the final outcome.[4] In addition, this approach explains why the level of dissatisfaction might be compounded in many cases. According to this model, many litigants do not appeal because they become convinced that all courts would use the same unfair procedures that they believe they encountered in the trial court; as defined by the similar court/same outcome conception of the appellate court. Such litigants are likely to have greater hostility toward the courts in general because, by definition, they believe that all courts are unfair in their treatment of litigants. This idea might explain the current finding that the greater the level of interaction with the courts by litigants, the less supportive many litigants feel toward the courts in general (Yankelovich, Skelly, and White 1977; Fossati and Meeker 1995). Such litigants are more likely to express their hostility toward the courts than they are to direct such hostility toward the opposing party. The opposing party is considered less liable for the current dilemma in which the losing litigants find themselves than is the court, which the litigants view as the source of the current injustice through its use of an unfair process to determine their case. Consequently, litigants turn their ire on the judges and other court personnel who they believe are the true source of their current dissatisfaction.

Explaining Legitimacy

To date, legitimacy has been a problematic category for scholars who have approached it from the outcome-based perspective. Legitimacy is hard to understand when scholars assume that people prefer to win. The assumption is that support accrues to the institution only from those parties that win in that institution and only as long as the parties continue to win. For example, Gibson et al. (1997, 30) argued that "courts become known to their constituents by making decisions pleasing to them. As satisfaction accumulates, a more enduring allegiance to the institution develops—that is, the institution acquires legitimacy."[5] The source of the support is identified as the fact that the institution allows the parties to win. Such an approach is comparable to the goodwill that one might generate for the blackjack dealer who brings one luck by turning over the correct cards. According to the outcome-based approach, one's support for such a person runs only as deep as the winning streak. Consequently, the courts have been identified as accruing legitimacy from those parties who receive a number of positive decisions from them, such as federalists at the start of the United States, industrialists at the turn of the twentieth century, and African Americans during the post–Second World War era (McCloskey 1994). But it has been assumed that such legitimacy exists only while the courts continue to shower the specific groups with positive decisions. As soon as the courts are identified as offering a series of negative decisions, it is assumed that they lose legitimacy in the face of such groups. In making these negative decisions, which lose the courts the support of one group, the courts may simultaneously develop alternative sources of legitimacy from the new beneficiaries of the positive decisions. Each group that does not "win" in the court is identified as alienated from the courts, and such groups are posited as identifying the courts' authority as illegitimate. In this context, it is assumed that the courts can only afford to alienate so many groups at one time if they are to maintain enough legitimacy to function. Consequently, the courts have been reluctant to consider more than a few controversial issues at any one time (Dahl 1957; McCloskey 1994).

Such an approach has difficulty explaining the long-term allegiance of groups to the courts even if those groups are not the current beneficiaries of positive decisions. It is this aspect that the process-based approach could help to explain in regard to the notion of legitimacy. According to the process-based approach, the legitimacy of the courts as institutions depends on the perceptions and expectations of the fairness of their process rather than on the fact that some litigants win. In those cases in which the courts are considered to use a fair process in deciding disputes, litigants might place their long-term allegiance with such institutions, independently of their subsequent success rate in terms of outcomes. For example, we do not consider elections as valid only as long as the person whom we voted for in that election wins. Instead, we accord elections some legitimacy because they are thought to embody a fair process even if the outcomes do not always favor us. Similarly, the courts accrue legitimacy because of their identification as fair institutions even if the subsequent outcomes might go against the favored policy. The assumption is that the final decision was reached in a fair manner and after consideration of the various arguments, and therefore the court as an institution is legitimate even if we are not pleased by the subsequent outcome.

Tyler proposed that if people "regard legal authorities as more legitimate, they are less likely to break any laws, for they will believe that they ought to follow them, regardless of the potential for punishment" (Tyler 1990, 4). Tyler's proposition is that perceived legitimacy leads to compliance even if the person does not believe in the resultant law. In such a case, the person obeys the law, not because they believe in it or they fear punishment, but because they believe in the institution and/or the process that created that law. In the current case, the fact that some litigants believed that either the trial court was fair or that the appellate court would be fair reveals that it is possible for litigants to use the courts and suffer a loss while still identifying the overall institution as legitimate. However, such a proposition is to be considered only if we recognize the litigants as interested in more than winning and losing and we are willing to allow that individuals' assessment of the fairness of the process itself used by an institution can be closely linked to their subsequent perception of legitimacy . The process-based approach facilitates the notion that the legitimacy of the court is intimately linked to individuals' court experiences in terms of process (Casper 1978; O'Barr and Conley 1985; Tyler, Casper and Fisher 1989; Tyler 1990, 1994; Shamir 1990; Tyler and Rasinski 1991; Fossati and Meeker 1995).

This idea—that the legitimacy of the court is linked to the procedural perceptions and expectations of the litigants—works well in the converse case to explain why increased interaction with the court could lead many litigants to create a negative perception of the courts in general. In the current sample, those litigants in the similar court/same outcome version clearly represented a group of losing litigants whose level of dissatisfaction could be identified as having a subsequent impact on their perceptions and expectations of the courts in general. These litigants not only were dissatisfied by their current experience but clearly expected all subsequent court experiences to be similarly dissatisfactory. Since these litigants must have had some level of positive expectation about the courts' ability to resolve their dispute in order to become involved in the courts in the first place, this group can clearly be defined as a group whose use of the court has led to a subsequent decline in their perception of the legitimacy of the courts in general. After their court experience, they left the courts believing that all courts used an unfair process in deciding cases; a proposition that would directly undermine their allegiance to the courts' decisions and ultimately undermine the long-term legitimacy of the courts.

From this perspective, legitimacy relates directly to the perceived fairness of the process rather than the fact that one wins in the court. Further, legitimacy could still accrue to the courts in those situations in which one party consistently loses, as long as that party is convinced that the process is fair. Such an idea raises the proposition that the courts need not greatly fear the prospect of diminishing their legitimacy through alienating those groups who consistently lose in the courts. Instead, the courts are free to generate negative decisions to many groups as long as these decisions are identified as being reached in a fair manner. The greatest potential source of danger to the courts' legitimacy lies in the prospect that the courts are identified as not deciding cases through a fair process. Interestingly enough, such a prospect is more likely to arise if the courts fail to consider whole classes of cases because they fear for the subsequent impact on their legitimacy. In such cases, the courts will be considered as unfair because they have ignored a certain type of case in their desire to maintain their legitimacy.

The Prospect of Invisible Barriers

This new perspective on individual behavior requires a new focus by legal scholars on the relationship of individuals to the legal system. For example, consistent with the outcome-based approach, achieving equal access to the law has primarily been approached by both the courts (*Gideon v. Wainwright* 372 U.S. 335 [1963]) and legal scholars (Fisher and Ivie 1971; Galanter 1974; Auerbach 1976; Erlanger 1978; Abel 1979; Katz 1982; Olson 1984) by proposing the expansion of the access of all potential litigants to lawyers and legal resources independent of their financial means. The premise of such an approach has been that, if both parties possess relatively equal legal resources, the subsequent legal action will be fair; that is, the outcome will not be determined by the relative wealth of either party or their ability to use that wealth to their advantage in regard to legal resources. Galanter (1974, 144) proposed that such an equalization might "create many situations in which *both* [emphasis in original] parties were organized to pursue their long-run interest in the litigation arena."

The process-based approach raises the potential problem with the proposition that providing equal access to lawyers and legal resources is synonymous with an equalization of the distribution of justice. Within this proposition is the assumption that the only barriers to effective use of the legal system by many parties is their lack of legal resources. Consequently, the provision of additional legal services dissolves any barriers to equal use of the legal system. The process-based approach raises the possibility of additional barriers, beyond the overt lack of legal resources or the differences in financial resources.

Within the process-based approach, the litigants' perceptions and expectations of the fairness of the legal system were an important determinant of their subsequent decision whether to use the legal system. Consequently, these perceptions and expectations of the fairness that they should expect should they enter the legal arena may represent an "invisible barrier" that, independently of access to legal resources, precludes many litigants from continuing (or beginning) to use the court system. More important is the fact that such perceptions and expectations are linked to litigants' social characteristics. This last aspect could lead to a plausible scenario in which, notwithstanding sufficient legal resources, a whole group of people "chooses" not to use the court system based on the expectation that it will not be treated fairly by the courts. For example, the legal system could drastically improve the current access of working-class people to the courts through increasing free access to legal resources (e.g., Katz 1982), but working-class people could choose not to use such resources because they expect that they will be treated unfairly by the courts.

This last example raises the possibility that a court might appear prima facie to be fair and accessible based on outcomes but could actually discriminate against a group of people based on the message that it sends out to them. For example, the courts might clearly discourage a certain class of people based on their correctly perceived message that, if they choose to use the court, they will not be treated fairly. Thus, it is possible to have a legal system that appears fair but in which one group does not use the legal system because it correctly perceives that the legal system is unfair to it. This scenario appears especially invidious because it is easier to discern discrimination based on outcome than discrimination based on individual perceptions and expectations. For example, it is relatively easy to measure the success rates of two different types of groups and compare the difference of their means. In contrast, the perceptions and expectations of individuals are relatively amorphous elements that are closely linked to their culture and socialization. In addition, individual perceptions and expectations are very hard to transfer to an aggregate level to determine a pattern that might reveal a cultural bias, especially in those cases in which there is no apparent difference in outcomes. In such a case, a court could point to the fact that should a certain group of people choose to use the court, they would receive justice as documented by similar outcomes, but such documentation would belie the reality of the court experience for those individuals who chose to use the court to resolve their disputes.

In such a case, if one examined the decisions of the court, one would find no distinction between groups. Yet, during the course of the trial, different groups could be treated very differently such that the court clearly

sent the message that the judiciary was not an appropriate arena for the resolution of such disputes. For example, if the courts in the South of the
United States in the 1930s were considered, it might be that even if the
courts were seen to have given equal outcomes to both black and white litigants, the courts still could have discouraged African Americans from litigating by treating them in an unequal fashion in terms of process.

From such a perspective, the absence of certain groups, such as working-class people, women, or African Americans, from the appellate arena
might not be an issue that is resolved simply by extending their access to
legal resources. Independent of such resources, these potential litigants
might perceive correctly that the courts will not treat their claims in a fair
manner, and consequently, they would choose not to use the courts to
resolve their disputes.

In such a context, the importance of high-profile cases involving African Americans, such as the trial of the Los Angeles police officers in the
Rodney King assault case or the trial of O. J. Simpson, might be that they
allow other African Americans the means to gauge the courts' reactions in
order to fine-tune their expectations of how they would be treated by the
judiciary should they ever consider using the courts to resolve a dispute. In
the current interviews, many African American litigants mentioned the case
of Rodney King as evidence that they, as similarly situated people, could
not expect to be treated fairly by the courts. Such an idea occurred independently of the fact that their cases involved civil courts rather than criminal courts. For example, Appellant 37 (a thirty-seven-year-old man
involved in a custody case), when asked how the courts are viewed in general by people of a similar age, race, and income as himself, referred to the
Rodney King incident in this way:

> This last instance of, um, out in California . . . the young black men
> being beat and then saw the police get off scot free and, I mean, it
> just . . . it doesn't . . . seems like the laws and the systems are being fol-
> lowed as far as justice.

One other means for litigants to gauge the reactions of the courts in
regard to certain groups or classes of people might lie in the high media
profile offered to certain parts of the appointment process. Appointments
might be a means to signal that such groups are more likely or less likely to
receive a fair hearing of the issues in their claims. This is based on the

assumption that a person of similar characteristics is more able to empathize with the arguments of another similarly situated person; or, a person of similar characteristics will be able to represent the other similarly situated individuals' arguments in the policy-making process, because he will be more attuned to such arguments. In the current interviews, many litigants mentioned the composition of the courts in their statements in regard to aspects of the courts that either encouraged or discouraged them in regard to appealing.

The problem with such "invisible barriers" is that they can be equally manipulated by the courts in the opposite direction; that is, to convince litigants that they are receiving a fair process even if the outcomes demonstrate that one group is receiving a different response from the courts. Lind and Tyler (1988, 76) proposed that "it is certainly possible for the unscrupulous to design procedures that *appear* fair and *feel* [emphasis in original] satisfying even though they are not fair by objective standards." This raised the problem that litigants' subjective assessments could be based on a misrepresented version of reality—the specter of false consciousness or contradictory consciousness (see Marx and Engels 1965; Gramsci 1971, 333; Gramsci 1992; cf. Lukacs 1968; Moore 1978; Scott 1985, 1990). Such a problem is magnified in relation to expectations when the litigants have no real perceptions of the process on which to base their judgments and the litigants are dependent on their limited knowledge of the appellate court to assess the potential of their expectations' being manipulated by it.

Notwithstanding the various forms that such "invisible barriers" might take, the important aspect of these barriers for our purposes is that they can be considered only if legal scholars begin to examine the courts from the new perspective offered by the process-based approach. This approach demonstrates the necessity of considering the barriers to appealing as extending beyond the physical barriers, such as cost and delay, and incorporating cultural and perceptual barriers, such as individual or collective conceptions of the appellate courts and expectations of the treatment of similarly situated members of social groups. In looking at an institution, the process-based approach highlights the fact that important barriers to political action can be both visible and invisible to an interested third party. Yet it is clear that such barriers might have important consequences for how we assess the work of the courts in dispensing equal justice. To date, courts have been judged by their speed and efficiency in producing outcomes (e.g., Church and Heumman 1992) rather than by the more amorphous standards of the quality of their treatment of litigants or the messages that they project to the wider community (cf. Yankelovich, Skelly, and White 1977; Casper 1978; Casper, Tyler, and Fisher 1989). The value of the process-based approach lies in its call to examine the largely unconsidered aspects of the relationship of individuals to the courts, as well as its demand that legal scholars reexamine their traditional assumptions of those same relationships.

Conclusion

In this chapter, I offered a new perspective on many old issues, including why individuals appeal. To date, legal scholars have considered such issues from an outcome-based approach, and as I have demonstrated, their approach has hampered their ability to comprehensively explain many of the current issues regarding individuals in relation to the judiciary. The process-based approach offers a new perspective that allows legal scholars a fresh theoretical means through which to consider the ideas of appealing, compliance, court-related violence, and legitimacy. In addition, it offers the prospect that there might exist additional barriers to court usage than have been proposed traditionally.

The difference in the theoretical and practical implications of the two approaches has important policy consequences. Each year, the courts devote tremendous resources to these issues: resources to control the amount of appeals; law enforcement resources to ensure compliance with court decisions; security resources to limit court-related violence; and judicial resources to maintain the long-term legitimacy of the courts. In such a context, it matters which approach legal scholars adopt in considering these issues.

In this chapter, I have demonstrated that there are real advantages to considering such issues from the perspective offered by the process-based approach. This approach reintroduces the court as an entity and focuses the debate on the consequences of the process rather than on the outcome. Such an approach is in keeping with the ideas of the litigants, but it also has theoretical advantages that are yet to be reaped by legal scholars. The current study indicates that the time has come for legal scholars to adopt this new perspective in considering a wide range of individual behaviors in relation to the legal system.

5.

The Litigants, Their Lawyers, and the Two Approaches

Up to this point, I have treated the litigants as largely autonomous actors — free to pursue their own goals and beliefs. However, it should be evident that such a picture of the litigants subsumes the role of the lawyer as an influential counterpart to the litigant in most decisions about litigating. Throughout the book, the lawyer has been largely an absent figure. The lawyers appeared, alongside the legal system, as an important factor in determining the legal definitions of the litigants. Yet, up to this point, I have underplayed those elements that might highlight the influence that lawyers can exert over their clients in all aspects of litigating. I have largely reduced the lawyers' role to that of a more informed shadow of the litigants, but I have firmly left the site of the final decision-making process with the litigants themselves.

The current approach of subsuming the role of the lawyer is consistent with the legal literature, which, when considering decision making by individual litigants, treats lawyers as a more informed "alter ego" of the litigants (Johnson 1980–81, 570). From this viewpoint, the lawyers and the litigants are assumed to act as one entity, such that the lawyer is treated as simply an extension of how the litigant would act if he were better informed legally. Consequently, in the presentation of each approach in this book, I have treated the lawyers as though the "lawyers merely do what clients want or *would want if they understood what is at stake* [emphasis added]" (Johnson 1980–81, 568). Such an assumption is evident in the outcome- based approach, and it has been carried over into the present construction of a process-based approach until this point.

Yet such a picture of the lawyers' role in litigation fails to capture the full impact of lawyers on the litigants' decision-making processes. Further, while the two approaches offer a relatively similar definition of the role that lawyers play in regard to the litigant—for example, as important sources of information—they differ in their ability to offer explanations for some of the behavior displayed by litigants in their relationship to their legal representation. Therefore, in this section I reintroduce the lawyer into the consideration of both approaches, and I consider what each approach might offer in way of explaining litigants' behavior in relation to their legal representation.

Lawyers as Sources of Information

To date, sociolegal scholars have defined the role of lawyers using the outcome-based approach; that is, they have assumed that the role of lawyers is to ensure that their clients prevail in their claims (e.g., Rosenthal 1974; Cain 1979; Olson 1984; Griffiths 1986; Sarat and Felstiner 1986, 1988, 1989). From this perspective, they have treated the primary role of lawyers as involving three tasks: redefining individuals' claims into legal claims (e.g., Blumberg 1967, 20; Cain 1979; Felstiner, Abel, and Sarat 1981; Galanter 1983); predicting the likelihood of success of the litigants' claims (e.g., Sarat and Felstiner 1986, 127; Malsch 1989; Loftus and Wagenaar 1988; Jay 1989; Goodman 1992); and ensuring that litigants achieve that success (e.g., Olson 1984, 21–34) or, at least, ensuring that litigants recognize that it is not possible to achieve such success in the legal system (e.g., Sarat and Felstiner 1986, 127).

Therefore, in both approaches, lawyers are identified as an important source of information for the litigants. For example, Sarat and Felstiner (1986, 93) propose that "lawyers serve clients as important sources of information about legal rights, help clients relate legal rules to individual problems, and introduce clients to the way the legal process works." In an outcome-based approach, the lawyer possesses important information about the probability of a successful outcome, as well as the ability to transform the litigants' claims into the form necessary for successful resolution within the courts. Similarly, in the process-based approach, the lawyer possesses important information about the attributes and expected behavior of the appellate court. Such information allows the litigants to determine the likelihood of being treated fairly in the appellate court. In addition, lawyers are accorded the ability to articulate the litigants' claims in the best possible manner in order to ensure that the claims are understood correctly by the decision makers (e.g., Ziegler and Hermann 1972, 212).

However, the two approaches differ as to the nature of the most relevant information that lawyers provide to the litigants. Consistent with the premises of the outcome-based approach, scholars have focused on legal outcomes as the single defining characteristic relevant in any legal interaction. It has been assumed that the most important information that lawyers provide litigants is an estimate of the litigants' probability of receiving a positive outcome in relation to their current claim (Schuck 1986; Wittman 1988; cf. Rosenthal 1974). Using this information, it is assumed that litigants are able to determine whether they will be able to successfully obtain their desired goal by continuing their lawsuit. For example, Goodman (1992, 1) argues that "from the moment when a client first consults a lawyer until the matter is resolved, lawyers must establish goals in a case and estimate the likelihood that they can achieve these goals. In the course of litigation, lawyers constantly make strategic decisions or advise their clients based on their predictions about the outcome of the case."

In contrast, the process-based approach considers that the most important information that lawyers provide to their clients is about the procedures the litigants can expect to encounter in the courts. This aspect is twofold. First, lawyers provide information that allow litigants to interpret the actions of the trial courts. Consequently, the lawyers' information shapes the litigants' perceptions of their trial court experiences. In the current interviews,[1] the litigants consistently identified their lawyers as important and accurate sources of information about their trial court experiences. Second, lawyers provide information that allow the litigants to develop a conception of the appellate court; which, as we have noted, shapes the likelihood of the litigant subsequently appealing. The current interviews support the argument that lawyers helped shaped the litigants' expectations about the attributes of the appellate court and its likely behavior in regard to their claims.

The fact that lawyers command such an important position in regard to the litigants' access to information, as well as its subsequent interpretation, means that it is possible within the parameters established by both approaches for the lawyer to exercise a hegemonic influence over the decision of the losing litigant on whether to appeal. This phenomenon is often noted in the literature in regard to lawyer-client relations (e.g., Rosenthal 1974; Olson 1984; Griffiths 1986; Sarat and Felstiner 1986, 1988, 1989, 1995). Thus, the traditional argument in relation to lawyer-client relations is that the lawyer dominates the decision-making process of the litigant. In summarizing the existing literature in this area, Sarat and Felstiner (1995,

19–20) proposed that the "predominant image of the lawyer-client relationship is one of professional dominance and lay passivity. The lawyer governs the relationship, defines the terms of the interaction, and is responsible for the services provided. Even when lawyers seek to tell their clients' stories, they routinely silence and subordinate them." However, the degree of influence will be shaped by the nature of the individual lawyer-client relationship.

For example, in the current interviews, despite their admitted lack of legal knowledge, most lawyer-represented appellants felt that they were operating on a coequal basis with their lawyers when it came to the decision to appeal. However, as these examples demonstrate, the litigants ranged in position from the opinion that they were being influenced strongly by their lawyer's advice to the opposite end of the spectrum. But the median position was to assume that the decision was mutual.

> I was influenced a lot by what lawyer said. He has had more appellate experience. (Appellant 20: a forty-five-year-old woman involved in a marriage dissolution case)

> My husband [a layperson] controlled appeal. (Appellant 61: a thirty-six-year-old woman involved in a contractual dispute with an insurance company)

> I decided to appeal and [lawyer] encouraged me. (Appellant 54: a thirty-five-year-old woman involved in paternity action)

> I feel like [the lawyer] explained it to me. I mean, he can't explain something that somebody has never been through it, but . . . and . . . and I kind of pushed him some, because I wanted to know what was going on, and I wanted to be the one who knew first what was going on, and to be asked . . . I wanted to be involved in the decisions as they were going on, not to just have somebody doing the work and I'm a bystander. I'm a participant in this. And I had to kind of fight for that sometimes. (Appellant 71: a forty-six-year-old woman involved in a marriage dissolution action)

> Attorney was asked to appeal. Let's get it done. (Appellant 43: a sixty-nine-year-old man involved in a marriage dissolution case)

Overall, the two approaches do not differ significantly in regard to the relationship between litigants and their lawyers. Each approach assumes that lawyers are an important source of information. Further, although they differ on the information that lawyers provide to litigants, each approach recognizes that the fact that lawyers are such an important source of information for litigants facilitates the possibility that lawyers could dominate litigants' decision making. While the two approaches are similar in regard to the ability of the lawyers to intervene in the litigants' decision making, the two approaches differ in their ability to explain litigants' relationship to their legal representation.

In the next sections, I propose that the sociolegal literature indicates that lawyers operate using the assumptions of the outcome-based approach, while, as the current research demonstrates, their clients' goals are more consistent with the process-based approach. Such a disjuncture between litigant and lawyer helps to explain the literature on lawyer-client relations that notes that lawyers spend part of their time in "teaching" litigants the correct approach to litigation. In addition, I argue that the process-based approach offers a new means to explain the decision of some appellants to self-represent.

The Differing Perspectives of Litigants and Their Lawyers

When considering the nature of decision making by individual litigants, scholars have treated the lawyer and litigant as one entity; however, these same scholars have recognized that the goals pursued by lawyers may not always be consistent with the goals advocated by the actual litigants whom the lawyers represent. Johnson (1980-81, 567) argued that "once a dispute reaches a law office it ceases to be the sole property of the disputants. From then on, the disputants' preferences may not determine decisions on such questions as whether to litigate and what settlement terms to accept."

The legal scholarship on the impact of legal representation on litigants' perceptions argues that litigants maintain an assessment of the nature of their dispute that is independent of the definition their lawyer applies to the same dispute (Rosenthal 1974; Cain 1979; Felstiner, Abel, and Sarat 1980-81; Mather and Yngvesson 1980-81; Olson 1984; Sarat and Felstiner 1986, 1988, 1989; Griffiths 1986; Erlanger, Chambliss, and Melli 1987; Monsma and Lempert 1992). "Clients bring many issues to the solicitor, expressed and constituted in terms of a variety of everyday discourses. The lawyer translates these, and re-constitutes the issues in terms of a legal discourse"

(Cain 1979, 335). Therefore, two separate definitions of the issues in a dispute arise: the litigant's definition and her lawyer's definition.

Such a difference in the definition of the salient issues is more than a difference in nomenclature; it reflects differences in the very conception of the dispute that the litigant is seeking to have the court resolve. If one goes into court to seek redress for the way she has been treated by another party, it matters what she identifies as the issues that require redress. Any court response that does not address the issues that she identifies as preeminent in her dispute will be defined as failing to resolve the original dispute. As long as this disjuncture exists, a litigant is motivated to seek a means to reconcile it in order that the issues in the dispute, as defined by the litigant, can be properly resolved by the court.

In the current interviews, all of the appellants generally stated that what they believed to be the primary issues in their case were not the primary issues before the trial court. Furthermore, the focus of the trial court on the latter in making its ruling did not seem to change the appellants' view of the primary issues in their cases. This perspective held for all 95 appellants. Independently of the legal system's definition of the salient issues in their claims, they remained steadfast in their original perception of the important issues in their cases. They wanted the court to deal with these issues even if they were not the legal issues before the court. They sought affirmation of their perception of the important issues. If appellants thought they were in the right before they began their trial court actions, the decisions of the trial court to the contrary did nothing to sway such an opinion. In some cases, it almost seemed to consolidate their belief.

Conjecture on the Origins of This Difference and Possible Implications

Although the research is far from conclusive on this point, one potential explanation for this difference in perspectives might be that the approach adopted by the lawyers and the approach adopted by the litigants are consistent with the distinction between the outcome-based approach and the process-based approach, respectively. Based on the presentation of lawyers in the sociolegal literature, it appears that lawyers adopt an outcome-based approach. For example, Loftus and Wagenaar (1988, 441) proposed that "a lawyer considers the probable outcomes of further litigation steps and weighs them against economic benefits that are likely to be obtained without further litigation." In direct contrast, the current interviews demonstrate that the litigants adopt a process-based approach.

This difference in approaches, such that lawyers and their clients are actually considering the legal system from contradictory premises, might explain the widespread literature on the need for lawyers to "educate" their clients (e.g., Sarat and Felstiner 1986, 1988, 1989; Griffiths 1986; Sarat and Felstiner 1995). For example, Sarat and Felstiner (1986, 126) proposed that lawyers resolve this disjuncture between their perspective and that of their clients by teaching their clients the *correct* approach to the legal system: "Because lawyers' experience is so much more extensive than that of clients, lawyers attempt to 'teach' their clients about the requirements of the legal process and to socialize them into the role of the client" (Sarat and Felstiner 1986, 126).

It may be that such activity reflects on the fact that the litigants, based on their greater focus on procedural aspects of their court experience, might be responding to different cues and seeking a different goal than that offered to them by their lawyers, who are trained to view the case primarily in terms of outcome. When they are unable to "teach" their clients the *correct* approach, lawyers will often resort to other strategies to reconcile such differences in perspectives. The litigants are treated as "naive" actors who insist on introducing aspects of the case into the legal interaction that are inconsistent with a successful outcome (Sarat and Felstiner 1986, 130). Lawyers rectify such behavior by acting on the assumption that the litigants actually desire a similar goal to that pursued by the lawyer, despite the litigants' statements to the contrary. From this perspective, lawyers "may conclude, therefore, based on experience, that the client who demands vindication today will want a larger financial settlement and a smaller lawyer's bill tomorrow" (Sarat and Felstiner 1986, 126).

Given this difference in perspectives, there are two potential methods of resolving this disjuncture if one stays within the court system. The first method is for the litigant to force her lawyer to present the issues in the dispute in the way she defines them, in contrast to the lawyer presenting the issues in the dispute in the way the legal system categorizes them. However, we might assume that most lawyers would be reluctant to pursue such a course on the grounds that raising issues that are not consistent with the existing legal parameters is likely to be to the eventual legal detriment of their client (e.g., Olson 1984, 28–34, 139–43). However, this may explain why many of the litigants who appealed mentioned the fact that they had "shopped" their way through several lawyers in order to find one who would take their case on their terms.

The second method would be for the litigant to self-represent, because self-representation allows the litigant to choose which issues are presented to the court for resolution. Therefore, self-representation may be the only means available to the litigant to ensure that her issues are placed before the court for resolution. The interviews reveal that the appellants, whether self-represented or lawyer-represented, believed that there was an incongruity between the issues they identified as important and the issues the legal system had identified as requiring resolution. However, the self-represented litigants had one advantage over their lawyer-represented counterparts. Self-represented litigants, through the choice to self-represent, had maintained the ability to place directly before the court the issues that they identified as most salient. These litigants were not restrained by the buffer placed between them and the court by their legal representation. While the self-represented litigants were able to actively achieve this result, their lawyer-represented counterparts were passively dependent on the court to focus on the issues that they identified as salient. In such a context, the statement from one self-representing litigant (Appellant 47) that the "best presentation is myself" has merit.

In contrast, the lawyer-represented litigants consistently complained about the fact that there was no means through which to introduce their ideas about the case into the court. For example, Appellant 71 (a forty-six-year-old woman involved in a marriage dissolution action) notes on three separate occasions (listed below) that there existed a buffer between her thoughts on the case and her ability to communicate these ideas to the trial court:

> I didn't feel like the legal profession or the court system had an adequate way to measure what it was that I was trying to express or communicate.

> I don't know where I can input my personality or my personal reflection of what's going on into the system. I mean, you can't just go up and talk to the judge. You have to do it through a ream of papers and a whole bunch of other stuff, through motions and all this other kind of stuff. I mean, it's all kind of once removed.

> I think in general people, ordinary people, feel like victims in court, whether they . . . simply because of the rules, the regulations, the paper-

work, *the inability to communicate except through a lawyer* [emphasis added], for all those reasons.

In the current cases, the nature of the legal process was such that the courts were forced to deal with those issues that self-represented litigants chose to place on their docket. In fact, courts generally acknowledge this fact by their consistent attempts to restrict the ability of self-represented litigants to use this avenue as a means of bringing irrelevant issues before the courts (e.g., issues that do not fit neatly within the current legal parameters) (Zeigler and Hermann 1972; Mueller 1984). Although the courts retain the ability to reject the self-represented litigant's claims (as they retain the ability to reject the lawyer-represented litigant's claims), such rejections still occur in the context of the self-represented litigant forcing the court to examine those issues that the litigant chooses.

Even if, because of her decision to self-represent, the court subsequently refuses to hear her claim, there is virtually no disadvantage for the litigant in pursuing this strategy as long as the disjuncture over the salient issues exists. There is no benefit to the litigant if the court proceeds to focus on those issues that the litigant identifies as peripheral to her original dispute. After all, the litigant is not only a relevant party to the dispute, but she must also comply with the court's resolution. If the litigant is using the court to resolve a dispute (Merry and Silbey 1984), the failure of the court to recognize that dispute correctly, as the litigant views it, creates a situation in which the purpose of the litigation can be recovered only if the litigant has the means to reintroduce the issues of the original dispute into the discourse. Self-representation is one means of literally forcing the court to deal with the issues that the litigant defines as requiring court action to resolve. In this context, self-representation can be identified as a sound strategy in terms of the litigant's goals.

The fact that self-representation can, in such cases, be identified as a sound strategy does not always mean it is a successful legal strategy in terms of outcome. In the current instance, self-represented litigants chose to place the issues that they identified as most important before the court, independently of the court's subsequent reaction and even when self-representation possibly worked to their eventual legal detriment. It appears that the short-term advantage of redefining the legal focus of their case might have been purchased at the expense of the long-term legal consequences. Although self-representation gives the litigant the ability to restrict the legal transformation of her issues, the result of such control may be that the litigant is no longer able to fit her claim with the existing legal parameters. In the current interviews, those self-represented litigants who acknowledged that their claim was no longer consistent with the current legal parameters argued that the law should be altered in the future to incorporate such situations. Such a finding need not automatically be defined as evidence of an unsound legal strategy, since such litigants are merely seeking a change in the existing precedents. Consider the famous case of *Gideon v. Wainwright* 372 U.S. 335 (1963). By self-representing, Gideon was able to raise an issue that was inconsistent with the existing legal parameters: the constitutional question of his right to an attorney supplied by the state—a right that did not exist at that time. It was only by raising such an issue in the courts that Gideon was able to question and change those existing legal parameters (Lewis 1964). It appears that some of the self-represented litigants in the current interviews were asking for similar treatment.

Such a possible explanation for the decision of some litigants to self-represent is interesting, given that at least one in every five court actions (Zeigler and Hermann 1972, 159; cf. New York State Bar Association 1988, 572) is initiated by a litigant who is self-represented (pro se) rather than lawyer-represented. The traditional theory is that self-representation is forced on litigants by financial necessity and, if circumstances were otherwise, such self-represented litigants would always choose to be represented by a lawyer. This theory assumes that legal representation is essential to the effective articulation of the issues at the heart of the litigant's claim and that, without such legal representation, the court would be unable to decipher the litigant's claim sufficiently to resolve the dispute. From this perspective, it is argued that the decision to self-represent effectively precludes the litigant from ever establishing the legal credibility of her case and that "summary dismissal is often the most merciful course in such cases. . . . Even though this may lead to the rejection of a good claim because of the pro se litigant's inability to adequately articulate his claim, at least the rejection is rapid" (Zeigler and Hermann 1972, 212).

Based on this theory, court systems have increased legal restrictions on self-representation (Ziegler and Hermann 1972; Mueller 1984; New York State Bar Association 1988) and have increasingly used standby counsel (Wright 1984; Wright 1993; Young 1984) in an attempt to convince self-represented litigants that legal representation, while not necessarily inexpensive, is their only opportunity for a successful completion of their case (Carrizosa 1982; Mueller 1984; McCoin 1993). Since the courts identify that legal representation is essential to the effective articulation of the issues in a claim, the claims of self-represented litigants are defined as synonymous with frivolous lawsuits (Mueller 1984; Kulat 1984; Carrizosa 1992).

While contrasting with the traditional perspective on why some litigants self-represent, the current theory does have some support in the legal literature as well as case law. Self-representation has recently been identified as a self-affirming experience that many litigants might select precisely because of the personal empowerment that arises from maintaining control over the elements of their case. For example, the United States Supreme Court recognized in *Faretta v. California* 422 U.S. 806 (1975) that, regardless of the availability of competent legal counsel, some litigants choose to represent themselves even if such self-representation is to their eventual legal detriment (Robbins and Herman 1976, 630; Friedman 1990). This position was extended in *McKaskle v. Wiggins* 52 U.S.L.W. 4176 (1984), in which Justice O'Connor, writing for the Court, held that "the right to appear pro se exists to affirm the dignity and autonomy of the accused and to allow the presentation of what may, at least occasionally, be the accused's best possible defense" (as quoted in Young 1984, 112). These cases did not challenge the assertion that many litigants are forced to self-represent to avoid the additional financial burden associated with retaining legal counsel. Instead, these Supreme Court cases raised the proposition that self-representation might also occur because of its self-affirming impact on the litigants. Of course, self-representation could have an affirming effect on the litigant even if the litigant is initially forced into self-representation by the financial cost associated with retaining legal counsel.

In a similar approach, Joselson and Kaye (1983) argued that women who choose to self-represent in their marriage dissolution cases were often empowered because "they *themselves* [emphasis in original] were in control of the legal process which eventually led to their divorce decree; the process was neither as complicated nor as mysterious as they had imagined; and, as a result of having mastered this relatively straightforward legal task, they felt better about themselves and more competent in other areas of their lives as well" (Joselson and Kaye 1983, 245). This empowerment occurs because litigants feel that, by self-representing, they maintain control over the legal process as it relates to them. Under the parameters of legal representation, litigants surrender their control over their case to their lawyer and become "passive" actors in the process (Rosenthal 1974). "When the lawyer assumes the responsibility of acting for the client's interests, he or she is encouraged by existing law to impute stylized ends to the client rather than discerning the true, personal ends of the individual client" (Olson 1984, 140). In contrast to this passivity, self-representation is identified as a means to maintain control over all aspects of one's case (and in Joselson and Kaye's terms, over one's life). Such a proposition is consistent with the general importance attributed in the procedural justice literature to one's ability to have a "voice" in the decision-making process in regard to those decisions that most affect one (Thibaut and Walker 1975; Tyler 1988a, 1988b; Lind and Tyler 1988; Lind, Kanfer, and Earley 1990).

Viewing the act of self-representation as allowing the litigants to control the nature of their input into the policy-making process is consistent with the parameters of the process-based approach. In fact, it should not be surprising that, in approaching a policy-making institution, some people prefer to put their own case forward for their preferred policy—much as some protesters and lobbyists prefer to speak for themselves rather than through mediators. Further, such a position is only enhanced when there appears to be such a clear disjuncture between the approach of the lawyers and the approach of the litigants.

Overall, the current research is not sufficient to offer evidence about either the notion that the disjuncture between lawyers and their clients rests on their differing approach or the notion that some cases of self-representation represent an attempt to resolve this disjuncture. Yet the process-based approach lends credence to both of these notions. Consequently, it develops new ways of examining and explaining the relationship between lawyers and their clients.

Conclusion

To a large extent, the two approaches do not differ significantly in regard to the relationship between litigants and their lawyers. Each approach assumes that lawyers are an important source of information. Although they differ on the information that lawyers provide to litigants, each approach recognizes that the fact that lawyers are such an important source of information for litigants facilitates the possibility that lawyers could dominate litigants' decision making, a point that is also consistently highlighted in the literature concerning lawyer-client relations.

However, while a large difference is not apparent between the two approaches in terms of the relationship between lawyers and litigants, the process-based approach raises new possibilities for explaining some of the current behavior evident in the interactions of lawyers with litigants, as well as litigants with the courts. As was shown in the last chapter, the real value of introducing this alternative approach lies in its ability to offer new insights into individual behavior, as well as a new framework from which to approach such issues. In the current context, this new framework offers the possibility of insights into the lawyer-client relationship, but such insights definitely require extensive research before we can come to rely on them.

6.

Conclusion

In this final chapter, I consider the implications that arise from the relationship between the traditional approach and the alternative approach that I have suggested in this book. In addition, I will discuss the overall contribution of this book to the field of law and social science.

The Relationship between the Two Approaches

I argued that the process-based approach was more consistent with the ideas of litigants involved in the decision whether to appeal. Further, I proposed that the process-based approach offered legal scholars a better theoretical basis from which to understand the relationship of individuals to the judiciary. In doing so, I argued that the outcome-based approach, from which legal scholars have considered these issues traditionally, is flawed in its ability to explain the decision whether to appeal. And, if these two approaches were not related, this would be the end of the story. However, such a simple ending is thwarted precisely because of the nexus between these two antithetical approaches.

Because the two approaches are antithetical, they must be considered as equal counterparts in their ability to offer a theoretical framework through which to understand individual behavior. This introduces a new idea as to how scholars should attempt to understand the behavior of individuals in their interactions with institutions. To date, scholars have focused on the outcome-based approach. The current study demonstrates the validity and usefulness of a process-based approach. Yet both approaches are equally valid means for understanding individual behavior, and both approaches should be treated as equally potential means to explore examples of individual decision making.

Consequently, while empirical research can demonstrate that one approach, such as the process-based approach, might be more valid in the context of certain individual behavior, such as the decision whether to appeal, this finding does not invalidate the overall usefulness of the other approach; it only questions its application in that particular context at that particular time. Instead, scholars should begin from the notion that each approach offers an equally likely means to explain individual behavior in a variety of contexts. The real determinant of which approach is more applicable in any particular context at any particular time will depend on a range of factors, including an individual's perceptions and expectations of the potential for bias within an institution.

In the current example of the decision whether to appeal, it is possible that the process-based approach is more consistent with the ideas articulated by litigants precisely because it offers them a more readily accessible means of determining whether there is bias in the courts. To determine bias in the courts in terms of outcome, one must compare a variety of outcomes to one's own outcome in relation to some notion of distributive justice. Such a comparison requires that individuals compare the outcome of the cases of similarly situated individuals to determine whether their case was treated differently. Practically, this might not be an easy comparison to engage in for litigants who have just completed their cases in the trial court. It requires a great deal of knowledge that the litigants may not be able to access.[1] In contrast, it might be easier and more practical for individual litigants to measure the possibility of bias in terms of process than it is for them to measure it in terms of outcome. Assessing the fairness of the process requires the litigant to engage in an assessment of the immediate procedures that they encounter as a normal part of their court experience, and such an assessment might require less knowledge than would a similar assessment as part of the outcome-based approach. Consequently, it could be true that the process-based approach is more consistent with the ideas of the litigants simply because the approach is a more readily accessible means by which the litigants can access the courts' activities. Further, the process-based approach may offer a better explanation of the individual's behavior more as a consequence of its accessibility than for any other reason. In such a context, the process-based approach would be used in those cases in which the necessary information for its use was more readily accessible to individuals than was the information required by the outcome-based approach. This scenario represents the possibility of the chosen approach being a reflection of the ability to access information rather than the grandeur of the theoretical basis.

In a similar vein, it is also possible that the process-based approach is a valid explanatory approach only in those contexts in which individuals begin with the predisposition that the process is likely to be biased. As long as such a predisposition exists, individuals are likely to favor a process-based approach because it highlights those factors that are designed to consider whether the process really is biased. Such a proposition is consistent with the behavior and ideas of the litigants in the current interviews. In such a case, the process-based approach would be the correct theoretical basis for considering the activities of individuals only as long as this predisposition exists. In any context in which the individuals do not begin with such a predisposition, the outcome-based approach might offer a better theoretical basis for understanding the behavior of individuals in regard to the institution of the courts. The trouble is that one could never be quite sure when such a shift in attitude might occur. Consequently, even though the current interviews favor the process-based approach, it is possible that, in other arenas or in other time periods, the outcome-based approach would be more consistent with the ideas of the litigants, because in that arena or at that time, they would be less predisposed to believe that the process is biased.

Finally, it is possible that the process-based approach is more consistent with the ideas of individual litigants involved in civil cases, but such an approach might not be consistent with the approach adopted by individuals in other parts of the legal system; for instance, judges and lawyers. Research seems to indicate that judges (e.g., McCoin 1993) and lawyers (e.g., Kritzer 1991) are more likely to view cases in terms of the outcome. In such a scenario, lawyers and judges might adopt the outcome-based approach in considering cases and they might attempt to apply such an approach to defining the litigants' best interests. Therefore, the outcome-based approach might be a better explanation for understanding most litigation strategies and the determination of cases, independently of whether it is the approach that is most consistent with the ideas of the individual litigants.

What is important is that the two approaches, while antithetical, represent equally valid possible approaches that can be used to explain the behavior of individuals. However, while the two are equally valid approaches to understanding individual behavior, the best possible explanation at any time will depend on the nexus between these two approaches. Any hint of bias will cause the individuals to substitute one approach for its complement. In such instances, the correct approach to be used at any time depends on a range of factors, such as the predisposition of the individuals and their ability to access certain information, that has little to do with the explanatory power of each approach. Rather, the approach adopted has more to do with the circumstances that the researcher might encounter in particular institutions at particular times.

Because it is dependent on perceptions and expectations about institutions, the approach adopted by individuals might vary along several cleavages. For example, it is possible that about half of individuals focus on the process in assessing the institution's behavior because these individuals are predisposed by socialization to expect that the courts are likely to be biased. At the same time, the other half might focus on the outcome because their different socialization has predisposed them to the viewpoint that the courts are highly unlikely to be biased. In this context, both approaches would be equally explanatory.

The interesting aspect of such cleavages might occur in regard to differences in race, gender, or class. For example, it is possible that the historical prejudice against one group of individuals by an institution might mean that those individuals are more likely to suspect the presence of bias in relation to subsequent interactions with that institution (e.g., Major et al. 1989; Hirsch 1989). At the same time, other individuals who are not members of that group might be less likely to suspect the presence of bias in their own subsequent interactions with the same institution. In relation to the American judiciary, which has a long history of racist and sexist decisions, we might conjecture that African Americans and women would be more likely to suspect the presence of bias in such courts than would many of their white male counterparts. Consequently, it is not surprising that, in the current study, many litigants referred to their social characteristics as an indicator of how they expected the court to subsequently treat them.

Thus, while I have worked in this book to demonstrate the value of adopting a process-based approach to explaining the decision to appeal, the very relationship between the two approaches to individual behavior raises the possibility that the explanatory preeminence of the process-based approach in the current question might be temporary or context-dependent. If so, it is harder now to make the claim that the process-based approach is the better means by which to always explain the decision to appeal. However, the real value of this book can be taken as the demonstration of the validity of the process-based approach as a framework to explain individual behavior, as well as the recognition that there exists an antinomy in regard to framing how we understand individual behavior. Therefore, if there is one thing that this book might accomplish, it is to accord the process-based approach its place as the rightful complement to the outcome-based approach, such that legal scholars might consider the theoretical ideas offered by both approaches when beginning to examine the behavior of individuals in relation to the legal system. To date, legal scholars have adopted a one-sided view of such behavior. It is my hope that the current text offers the foundation for balancing that view.

In this book, I considered why some individuals appeal their loss in civil court while other similarly situated individuals do not appeal. While most legal scholars argue that individuals who have lost a civil court case appeal only if they stand a chance of winning, I demonstrated that the individuals' objective is to ensure fair treatment in an attempt to resolve their disputes. I argued that these two different assumptions about the motivation of individuals—the desire to win versus the desire to be treated fairly—form the basis of the two different approaches: the outcome-based approach and the process-based approach, respectively. These two antithetical approaches provide a framework for understanding individual behavior, including the decision to appeal. To date, legal scholars have focused almost exclusively on models from an outcome-based approach in order to explain the behavior of individuals in relation to the judiciary. Using the decision to appeal as an example, I demonstrated the validity of adopting models for individual behavior that are based on a process-based approach. I explored the outlines of such an approach, and I commented on its ability to offer an explanation, which is consistent with the behavior of individual civil litigants and the ideas that they articulate, for why some individuals appeal while their similarly situated counterparts do not.

In developing the relationship between these two approaches to individual behavior, I demonstrated that the approach adopted for understanding individual behavior subsequently frames how we define the actions of individuals and the means that we should employ to alter their behavior, if we so choose. Consequently, the approach used to understand individual behavior has widespread policy implications, and I proposed that the singular focus on the outcome-based approach might lead to legal scholars' misunderstanding the behavior of individuals, as well as offering potentially ineffective means for altering such behavior.

In developing the outlines of a process-based approach, I proposed that such an approach defines individuals as initiating appeals as a means of having input into the policy-making process. This input must be such that the ideas of those parties who are likely to be affected are heard and considered in a fair manner by those responsible for determining a final policy in this matter. This approach alters the traditional focus on winners and losers. Instead, it offers a more dynamic view of the role of the courts and the legal system, in which success is measured in terms of the seriousness with which one's ideas are considered in reaching decisions of relevance. I have argued that this more dynamic view, in which the process is a validating act in its own right, is consistent with the theoretical ideas raised by both Habermas (1996) and Dahl (1979) in their considerations of the basis of democratic systems. The implications of such an approach include the need for a reconsideration of how we define the activities of legal actors and the legal system.

Consistent with the move away from winners and losers, I also argued that the process-based approach offers a means by which to gain a new perspective on such issues as compliance, legitimacy, and court-related violence. These issues have represented paradoxes when approached from a traditional perspective with its focus on the outcome of cases. Instead, I proposed that the process-based approach offered the theoretical means by which to understand the basis of legitimacy and the subsequent logic for compliance and court-related violence. Further, I raised the possibility that equal access to the law could be precluded by the "invisible barriers" erected through the various messages that the courts send to different social groups.

In regard to lawyer-clients relations, I noted that, although the two approaches share many aspects of how they view the relationship between lawyers and litigants, the process-based approach offers the potential for new insights into some elements of this relationship. In the previous chapter, I considered the implications of the process-based approach as offering a framework for understanding the extensive literature on the need of lawyers to "teach" their clients. I proposed that this requirement arises because lawyers operate using the assumptions of the outcome-based approach, while their clients are adopting a process-based approach. In addition, I proposed that such a distinction in approaches may underscore the decision of some litigants to self-represent at the appellate stage.

In developing an alternative approach to individual behavior, I highlighted the fact the two approaches were antinomies. Each offered an equally valid framework for understanding individual behavior. Since each approach offered a potentially equally valid explanation of individual behavior in any context, I proposed that it is an empirical question that answers which approach is the better explanatory framework in any particular context.

Further, because of the divergent focus of these two approaches, they offer two different definitions of the meaning of justice. Although both approaches adopt justice as a means of measuring the validity of any individual's interactions with the legal institutions, the two approaches adopt differing definitions of justice. The outcome-based approach uses a notion of distributive justice, while the process-based approach uses a notion of procedural justice. Thus, it is important for legal scholars to recognize the divergence in the notions of justice that underscore the discussion of the validity of the acts of the judiciary.

Finally, while the current manuscript focuses on the decision to appeal, it is clear that the ideas raised in this book should apply to a variety of institutional interactions. In this book, I argued that individuals should be identified as more than self-interested actors. Following the lead of the theoretical ideas offered by Dahl (1979) and Habermas (1996), I have turned to process as a way to extricate the individual from the well-worn path trodden by so many legal scholars in regard to individual behavior. Instead, I have placed the individual on a new path in which the process offers a means for understanding individual behavior, as well as the means for placing such behavior in a collective or systemic context. It is my hope that a few more scholars will be enticed to try this alternate path to understanding why people behave as they do.

Sample Questionnaire

Date:

Interview number:

Identification number:

Hello. My name is Scott Barclay and I am an assistant professor at the State University of New York at Albany. The university is conducting a study of why people appeal. You should have recently received a letter that detailed our interest in interviewing you. As our letter mentioned, we simply want to find out how people involved in the process of appealing view this process. Your answers will be confidential and will have no impact on your case in any way.

1a. Please tell me about your case: how it started and why it went to court, anything *you* think is important.

1b. Did you originally file this case?

2. Were you surprised by the district court's verdict?

3a. What did you think of the way in which the district court reached a decision in your case?

3b. Were you satisfied with the procedures the district court used?

4a. Were you represented by a lawyer in the district court?

4b. Do you still have the same lawyer? (Or do you still represent yourself?)

4c. Tell me about your lawyer: Did he or she explain how your case would be handled by the district court? Did he or she tell you what to expect in the court? (Or why did you self-represent? If you did, how did you know what to expect in the district court?)

5. Who do you think exercised more influence in deciding that you should appeal, *you* or *your lawyer?* Why?

6. What stage are you currently at with your appeal?

7. Tell me a little about your appeal: why you brought it, what you hope to achieve, what you think of the appeals process, anything *you* think is important.

8. Tell me everything you know about the Mississippi Supreme Court.

9. How do you think the Mississippi Supreme Court will decide your case? What process will it use? What things do you think will be important?

10. Why do you think you need to appeal your case?

11. Do you think that you will get a better deal in the Mississippi Supreme Court than you got in the district court? Are there things about the supreme court that you thought would help your case?

12. Is there anything about the Mississippi Supreme Court that particularly attracted you when you thought about appealing?

13. Is there anything about the Mississippi Supreme Court that particularly discouraged you when you thought about appealing?

14. Can you think of *one* thing that would have caused you *not* to appeal?

15. Have you ever appealed before?

16. Before you considered appealing, had you heard much about the Mississippi Supreme Court?

17. What would you say the source of your current information on the Mississippi Supreme Court was?

18. Has everything you heard or learned about the Mississippi Supreme Court influenced you? How?

19. Why do you think that most people do not appeal their cases?

20. How much do you think your appeal will end up costing you?

21. Were you worried by the cost usually associated with appealing?

22. Please tell me your age, ethnic background, and income.

> *Age:*
>
> *Ethnic background:*
>
> *Estimated income:*

23. Do you think that the courts in general have been viewed positively or negatively by people of similar age, ethnic background, and income as yourself? What makes you think that?

Thank you very much for your time. The research is being used to gain new information about why people appeal. Your help is greatly appreciated and is very important to the study. As I mentioned in the letter, your comments will not be associated with your name or case in any way, and this interview has no impact on your case.

Notes

Chapter One

1. See, for example, in regard to tort reform: S 1400 and HR 2700 in 1990; S 640 and HR 3030 in 1991; S 687 and HR 1910 as well as PL 103-298 in 1994; S 565 and HR 956 in 1995; S 5, S 364, S 648 and HR 872 in 1996 and 1997.

2. Wanting to appeal and subsequently appealing are two different actions. In the current scenario, the litigants should want to appeal even if they subsequently do not or cannot appeal.

3. To accompany such an approach, a notion of neutral legal decision making has been promoted from time to time in the legal literature (Levi 1949; Weschler 1959; Bork 1971).

4. Certain cases were precluded by the courts from consideration as part of the sample. Court records involving adoption orders and child welfare, cases involving civil assault in the form of rape/sexual assault, cases involving civil claims involving a city's failure to protect in relation to rape/sexual assault in a city-owned facility, and cases involving sexual harassment were all removed from the sample by the courts as part of the author's agreement of access to the courts' documents.

5. Although the problem of individuals' self-reporting is clearly acknowledged (e.g., Nisbett and Wilson 1977; Konecni and Ebbesen 1982).

Chapter Two

1. In this regard, Posner's model lags behind the advances in the field of economics in terms of the issue of the calculation and use of nonmonetary goals—as evident, for example, in the recent work of Becker (1996).

2. Some individuals can be defined as repeat players. For example, in the criminal arena, prostitutes, habitual criminals, and homeless persons might be defined as repeat players because of their ongoing contact with the police and courts. However, there are no similar categories of individuals who might be defined as repeat players in the civil arena unless one incorporates "nuisance" filers who repeatedly file civil claims (e.g., Mueller 1984).

3. In fact, when each model is tested, it is found to be flawed in regard to the same issue: each defines the motivation of individuals as the desire to win. Since this is the point of commonality that all three models share, it seems more fitting that they are tested in terms of this common outcome-based approach (see Barclay 1993).

4. In some of the more "political" cases, certain other characteristics of the litigant were incorporated by theorists into the case, although such characteristics are not essential to court resolution. Notwithstanding the fact that a formerly pregnant woman initiated the landmark 1973 abortion case, subsequent cases are usually initiated by abortion clinics or doctors. See *Roe v. Wade, District Attorney of Dallas County* 410 U.S. 113 (1973); *Planned Parenthood v. Casey* 120 L.Ed. 2d 674. Similarly, non–African Americans have initiated important racial discrimination suits involving discrimination against African Americans. See *Peters v. Kiff* 407 U.S. 493 (1971).

5. Interestingly enough, this issue arose in Minnesota partially because the Minnesota Court of Appeals had chosen specifically to ride circuit; that is, to hear some cases while sitting in the original jurisdiction of the case. The court began riding circuit because it was assumed that such activity would be appreciated by the litigants since it brought the court geographically and, it was assumed, culturally closer to the litigants (see Popovich 1987).

Chapter Three

1. Janus is a figure from Greek mythology who, according to *Webster's New Twentieth Century Dictionary* (1970), "was guardian of portals and patron of beginnings and endings; he is shown as having two faces, one in front, the other at the back of his head, symbolizing his power."

2. *Brown v. Board of Education of Topeka, Kansas et al.* 347 U.S. 483 (1954). Although Brown was a minor, she still presumably had the power to end

her claim even if it were made on her behalf. Other similarly placed litigants had done so in the past (Kluger 1976).

3. There are two possible explanations for the manner in which the losing litigants' expectations parallel the legal definitions of the roles of the appellate court. First, losing litigants may be internalizing one of the scholarly conceptions of the roles of the appellate court as part of their preconceived expectations about the appellate court. Second, the losing litigants may be responding to the same cues as scholars in interpreting the role of the appellate court.

Chapter Four

1. Hence, as noted in chapter 2, Baum (1981) used this premise as a basis for his theory of why people appeal. Even though I take on parts of this differentiation of litigants as a basis for why individuals appeal, my theory differs from Baum's by rejecting the basic premises that compose the framework for his distinction between these two categories.

2. See, for example, *Guinn v. United States* 238 U.S. 347 (1915); *Nixon v. Herndon* 273 U.S. 536 (1927); *Nixon v. Condon* 286 U.S. 73 (1932); *Smith v. Allwright* 321 U.S. 649 (1944); and *Schnell v. Davis* 336 U.S. 933 (1949).

3. Kritzer (1984, 1991; Kritzer et al. 1985) has proposed that there are actually three identifiable categories in regard to outcome: prevailing, nonprevailing, and losing. It has been proposed that the losing category is composed of nonprevailing and losing parties: The losing party does not expect to lose, while the nonprevailing party did not expect to win and is merely seeking to minimize damage. In addition, in some cases, third-party interventions force the parties to a result in which each litigant views the outcome as a loss.

4. For a related example of how, after a process that is generally perceived as unfair, blame is attributed to decision makers rather to than the opposing party, consider the electoral response of the general public to the relevant senators after the Anita Hill segment of Clarence Thomas's Senate confirmation hearings (Littleton 1992; Curtin 1992; Schroeder 1992).

5. I am certainly not the first scholar to critique this basis for legitimacy from a process-based perspective. For example, see the ongoing debate between

Gibson and Tyler on this very issue (Gibson 1989, 1991; Tyler and Rasin-ski 1991; Tyler 1994; Tyler and Mitchell 1994).

Chapter Five

1. It should be remembered that 25 percent (31 out of 125) of the interviews were conducted with litigants who self-represented, while the remaining 75 percent (94 out of 125) were represented by legal counsel.

Chapter Six

1. Loftus and Wagenaar (1988, 450) argue a similar proposition in relation to lawyers' determining win ratios based on their own past experiences.

Works Cited

Abel, Richard L. 1979. "Socializing the Legal Profession: Can Redistributive Lawyers' Services Achieve Social Justice?" *Law and Policy* 1: 5–51.

Ackerman, Bruce A. 1980. *Social Justice in the Liberal State.* New Haven, Conn.: Yale University Press.

Adams, Edward A. 1990. "Security Incidents in State Courthouses Appear to Hold Steady." *New York Law Journal* 204 (September 19): p. 1.

Adams, J. S. 1963. "Toward an Understanding of Inequity." *Journal of Abnormal and Social Psychology* 67: 422–36.

Adler, J. W., D. R. Hensler, and C. E. Nelson. 1983. *Simple Justice: How Litigants Fare in the Pittsburgh Court Arbitration Program.* Santa Monica, Calif.: RAND Institute for Civil Justice.

Atkins, Burton. 1990. "Party Capability Theory as an Explanation for Intervention Behavior in the English Court of Appeal." *American Journal of Political Science* 35: 881–903.

———. 1993. "Alternative Models of Appeal Mobilization in Judicial Hierarchies." *American Journal of Political Science* 37: 780–98.

Atleson, James B. 1989. "The Legal Community and the Transformation of Disputes: The Settlement of Injunction Actions." *Law and Society Review* 23: 41–74.

Auerbach, Jerold S. 1976. *Unequal Justice.* London: Oxford University Press.

Baker, Lynn A., and Robert E. Emery. 1992. "When Every Relationship Is above Average: Perceptions and Expectations of Divorce at the Time of Marriage." Paper presented at the annual meeting of the Law and Society Association, Philadelphia, Pennsylvania. May 28, 1992.

Barclay, Scott W. 1993. *An Appealing Act*. Ph.D. dissertation. Evanston, Ill.: Northwestern University.

——. 1997a. "Posner's Economic Model and the Decision to Appeal." *Justice System Journal* 19: 77–100.

——. 1997b. "False Consciousness and the Rational Choice Perspective in Law and Economics." Paper presented at the annual meeting of the Canadian Law and Society Association, St. John's, Newfoundland. June 9, 1997.

Barrett-Howard, E., and Tom R. Tyler. 1986. "Procedural Justice as a Criterion in Allocation Decisions." *Journal of Personality and Social Psychology* 50: 296–304.

Baum, Lawrence. 1981. *The Supreme Court*. Washington, D.C.: Congressional Quarterly.

——. 1994. *American Courts*. Boston: Houghton Mifflin.

Becker, Gary S. 1996. *Accounting for Tastes*. Cambridge, Mass.: Harvard University Press.

Becker, Theodore, and Malcolm Feeley, eds. 1973. *The Impact of Supreme Court Decisions*, 2d ed. London: Oxford University Press.

Benn, Stanley I. 1988. *A Theory of Freedom*. Cambridge: Cambridge University Press.

Bennett, W. Lance. 1978. "Storytelling in Criminal Trials: A Model of Social Judgement." *Quarterly Journal of Speech* 64, no. 1: 1–22.

Bentham, Jeremy. [1789] 1948. *An Introduction to the Principles of Morals and Legislation*. Ed. J. H. Burns and H. L. A. Hart. London: Athlone Press.

Berg, Bruce L. 1989. *Qualitative Research Methods for the Social Sciences*. Boston: Allyn and Bacon.

Blau, Lauren. 1992. "Are the Courts Secure? Recent Incidents Are Spurring Debate on Improving Security Systems." *Los Angeles Daily Journal* 105 (August 20): 1.

Blumberg, Abraham S. 1967. "The Practice of Law as a Confidence Game: Organizational Cooptation of a Profession." *Law and Society Review* 1: 16–39.

Bork, Robert. 1971. "Neutral Principles and Some First Amendment Problems." *Indiana Law Journal* 47: 1–19.

Breiner, Peter. 1996. "Deliberative and Associative Democracy and the Problem of Power Struggle." Paper presented at the annual meeting of the American Political Science Association, San Francisco, California. September 6, 1996.

Brisbin, Richard A., Jr., and Susan Hunter. 1991. "Perceptions of Justice: Clientele Evaluations of Conflict Adjustment by a Utility Regulatory Agency." Paper presented at the annual meeting of the Law and Society Association, Amsterdam, The Netherlands. June 27, 1991.

Brooks, David. 1989. "Security Tightened after Threat to Hudson Judge." *New Jersey Law Journal* 124 (October 5): p. 5.

Cain, Maureen. 1979. "The General Practice Lawyer and the Client: Towards a Radical Conception." *International Journal of the Sociology of Law* 7: 331–54.

Carmichael, Stokely, and Charles V. Hamilton. 1967. *Black Power.* Middlesex, England: Penguin Books.

Carrizosa, Philip. 1982. "Weird Self-Representation Cases Troubles Supreme Court Justices." *Los Angeles Daily Journal* 95 (December 9): p. 2.

———. 1992. "Appeal Court Roasts Pro Per for Steakhouse Bias Suit." *Los Angeles Daily Journal* 105 (November 4): p. 2.

Casey, Jeff T., and John T. Scholz. 1991. "Beyond Deterrence: Behavioral Decision Theory and Tax Compliance." *Law and Society Review* 25: 821–43.

Casper, Jonathan D. 1978. "Having Their Day in Court: Defendant Evaluations of the Fairness of Their Treatment." *Law and Society Review* 12: 237–51.

Casper, Jonathan D., Tom R. Tyler, and Bonnie Fisher. 1988. "Procedural Justice in Felony Cases." *Law and Society Review* 22: 483–507.

Chapper, Joy A., and Roger A. Hansen. 1990. *Intermediate Appellate Courts: Improving Case Processing.* Final Report, National Center for State Courts, Washington, D.C.

Cheever, Joan M., and Joanne Naiman. 1992. "The Deadly Practice of Divorce." *National Law Journal* 15 (October 12): p. 1.

Church, Thomas. 1985. "Examining Local Legal Culture." *American Bar Foundation Research Journal* 1985: 449–518.

Church, Thomas, and Milton Heumann. 1992. *Speedy Disposition*. Albany, N.Y.: State University of New York Press.

Cleaver, Eldridge. 1968. *Soul on Ice*. London: Jonathan Cape.

Cohen, Joshua. 1989. "Deliberation and Democratic Legitimacy." Pp. 17–34 in *The Good Polity: A Normative Analysis of the State*, ed. Philip Pettit and Alan Hamilin. Oxford: Basil Blackwell.

Cohen, Ronald L. 1987. "Distributive Justice: Theory and Research." *Social Justice Research* 1, no. 1: 19–39.

Conley, John M., and William M. O'Barr. 1987. "Fundamentals of Jurisprudence: An Ethnography of Judicial Decision Making in Informal Courts." *North Carolina Law Review* 66: 467–507.

Cox, Archibald. 1976. *The Role of the Supreme Court in American Government*. Oxford: Clarendon Press.

Curtin, Dennis E. 1992. "The Fake Trial." *Southern California Law Review* 65: 1523–30.

Dahl, Robert A. 1957. "Decisionmaking in a Democracy: The Supreme Court as a National Policy-Maker." *Journal of Public Law* 6 (fall 1957): 279–95.

———. 1979. "Procedural Democracy." Pp. 97–133 in *Philosophy, Politics and Society: 5th Series*, ed. Peter Laslett and James Fishkin. New Haven, Conn.: Yale University Press.

Dalton, Harlon L. 1985. "Taking the Right to Appeal More or Less. Seriously." *Yale Law Journal* 95: 62–107.

Denzin, Norman K., and Yvonna S. Lincoln, eds. 1994. *Handbook of Qualitative Research*. Thousand Oaks, Calif.: Sage.

Dezalay, Yves, and Bryant Garth. 1995. "Merchants of Law as Moral Entrepreneurs: Constructing International Justice from the Competition for Transnational Business Disputes." *Law and Society Review* 29: 27–64.

Downs, Anthony. 1957. *An Economic Theory of Democracy*. New York: Harper and Row.

Durkin, Tom. 1991. "Framing the Choice to Sue: Victim Cognitions and Claims." *American Bar Foundation Working Paper Series*, no. 9119.

Eisenstein, James. 1978. *Counsel for the United States: U.S. Attorneys in the Political and Legal Systems*. Baltimore: Johns Hopkins University Press.

Erlanger, Howard S. 1978. "Lawyers and Neighborhood Legal Services: Social Background and the Impetus for Reform." *Law and Society Review* 12: 253-74.

Erlanger, Howard S., Elizabeth Chambliss, and Marygold S. Melli. 1987. "Participation and Flexibility in Informal Processes: Cautions from the Divorce Context." *Law and Society Review* 21: 585-604.

Ewick, Patricia, and Susan S. Silbey. 1995. "Subversive Stories and Hegemonic Tales: Toward a Sociology of Narrative." *Law and Society Review* 29: 197-226.

Feeley, Malcolm M. 1992. "Hollow Hopes, Flypaper, and Metaphors." *Law and Social Inquiry* 17: 745-60.

Felstiner, William L. F., Richard L. Abel, and Austin Sarat. 1980-81. "The Emergence and Transformation of Disputes: Naming, Blaming, Claiming." *Law and Society Review* 15: 631-54.

Fisher, Kenneth P., and Charles C. Ivie. 1971. *Franchising Justice: The Office of Economic Opportunity Legal Services Program and Traditional Legal Aid.* Chicago: American Bar Foundation.

Fossati, Thomas E., and James W. Meeker. 1995. "Evaluations of Institutional Legitimacy and Court System Fairness: A Study of Gender Differences." Paper presented at the annual meeting of the Law and Society Association, Toronto, Ontario. June 3, 1995.

Fox, Martin. 1987. "Added Security Steps Taken to Curb Outbreaks in Courts." *New York Law Journal* 198 (December 3): p. 1.

Friedman, Marc M. 1990. "People v. Bloom: The Trials of a 'Pro Per' Defendant." *Whittier Law Review* 11: 909-38.

Fuller, Lon L. 1981. "The Adversary System." Pp. 30-43 in *The Principle of Social Order: Selected Essays of Lon L. Fuller,* ed. Kenneth I. Winston. Durham, N.C.: Duke University Press.

Galanter, Marc. 1974. "Why the 'Haves' Come Out Ahead: Speculations on the Limits of Legal Change." *Law and Society Review* 9: 95-160.

———. 1983. "Reading the Landscape of Disputes: What We Know and Don't Know (and Think We Know) about Our Allegedly Contentious and Litigious Society." *UCLA Law Review* 31: 1-71.

———. 1993. "News from Nowhere: The Debased Debate on Civil Justice."
   Denver University Law Review 71: 77–113.

Gallet, Jeffry H. 1990. "Violence in the Courthouse." *New York Law Journal* 204
   (December 11): p. 2.

Garth, Bryant G. 1992. "Privatization and the New Market for Disputes: A Framework for Analysis and a Preliminary Assessment." *Studies in Law, Politics,
   and Society* 12: 389–413.

Geiger, Fred A. 1989. "Safety First: A Guide to Courthouse Security." *Judges Journal*
   28: 14.

Geras, Norman. 1985. "The Controversy about Marx and Justice." *New Left Review*
   150: 47–88.

Gibson, James L. 1989. "Understandings of Justice: Institutional Legitimacy, Procedural Justice, and Political Tolerance." *Law and Society Review* 23: 469–96.

———. 1991. "Institutional Legitimacy, Procedural Justice, and Compliance
   with Supreme Court Decisions: A Question of Causality." *Law and
   Society Review* 25: 631–35.

Gibson, James L., Gregory A. Caldeira, and Vanessa Baird. 1997. "On the Legitimacy of National High Courts." Paper presented at the annual meeting of
   the Law and Society Association, St. Louis, Missouri. May 30, 1997.

Giles, Michael, and D. Gatlin. 1980. "Mass Level Compliance with Public Policy:
   The Case of School Desegregation." *Journal of Politics* 42: 722–46.

Gizzi, Michael C. 1993. "Examining the Crisis of Volume in the U.S. Courts of
   Appeal." *Judicature* 77, no. 2 (September–October): 96–103.

Goodman, Jane. 1992. "Lawyer Overconfidence in Dispute Resolution." *Fund for
   Research on Dispute Resolution Summary Report*. Los Angeles, California.

Gordon, Michael E., and Gerald E. Fryxwell. 1989. "Voluntariness of Association as
   a Moderator of the Importance of Procedural and Distributive Justice."
   Journal of Applied Social Psychology 19: 993–1009.

Gosnell, Harold Foote. 1969. "Representative Democracy." Pp. 98–118 in *Representation*, ed. Hanna F. Pitkin. New York: Atherton.

Gramsci, Antonio. 1971. *Selections from the Prison Notebooks*. Tran. and ed. Quintin Hoare and Geoffrey Smith. New York: International Publishers.

———. 1992. *Antonio Gramsci: Prison Notebooks*. Vol. 1. Trans. and ed. Joseph A. Buttigieg. New York: Columbia University Press.

Griffiths, John. 1986. "What Do Dutch Lawyers Actually Do in Divorce Cases?" *Law and Society Review* 20: 135–75.

Habermas, Jürgen. 1996. *Between Facts and Norms: Contributions to a Discourse Theory of Law and Democracy*. Trans. William Rehg. Cambridge, Mass.: MIT Press.

Hamilton, Alexander. [1788] 1937. *The Federalist No. 78*. New York: Modern Library.

Hardenbergh, Don. 1993. "Justice without Fear: Are We Safe in Our Courthouses?" *State Court Journal* 17: p. 22.

Harrington, Christine B. 1985. *Shadow Justice: The Ideology and Institutionalization of Alternatives to Court*. Westport, Conn.: Greenwood Press.

Hart, H. L. A. 1941. *The Way to Justice*. London: Allen and Unwin.

———. 1961. *The Concept of Law*. Oxford: Clarendon Press.

Hirsch, Susan F. 1989. "Asserting Male Authority, Recreating Female Experience: Gendered Discourse in Coastal Kenyan Muslim Courts." *American Bar Foundation Working Paper Series*, no. 8906.

Hirsch, Werner Z., and Evan Osborne. 1992. "Law and Economics—Valuable but Controversial." *Law and Social Inquiry* 17: 521–37.

Howard, Woodford J. 1981. *Court of Appeals in the Federal Judicial System*. Princeton, N.J.: Princeton University Press.

Husami, Ziyad I. 1980. "Marx on Distributive Justice." Pp. 42–79 in *Marx, Justice, and History*, ed. Marshall Cohen, Thomas Nagel, and Thomas Scanlan. Princeton, N.J.: Princeton University Press.

Jay, Stewart. 1989. "The Dilemmas of Attorney Contingent Fees." *Georgetown Journal of Legal Ethics* 2: 813–84.

Johnson, Charles A., and Bradley C. Canon. 1984. *Judicial Policies: Implementation and Impact*. Washington, D.C.: Brookings Institute.

Johnson, Earl, Jr. 1980-81. "Lawyers' Choice: A Theoretical Appraisal of Litigation Investment Decisions." *Law and Society Review* 15: 567-610.

Johnson, Sue S., and Prakash Yerawadekar. 1981. "Courthouse Security." *Court Management Journal* 3: 8-12.

Joselson, Emily, and Judy Kaye. 1983. "Pro Se Divorce: A Strategy for Empowering Women." *Law and Inequality* 1: 239-75.

Katz, Daniel, Barbara A. Gutek, Robert L. Kahn, and Eugenia Barton. 1975. *Bureaucratic Encounters.* Ann Arbor, Mich.: Institute for Social Research.

Katz, Jack. 1982. *Poor People's Lawyers in Transition.* New Brunswick, N.J.: Rutgers University Press.

Kluger, Richard. 1976. *Simple Justice.* New York: Alfred A. Knopf.

Konecni, Vladimir J., and Ebbe B. Ebbesen. 1982. *The Criminal Justice System: A Social Psychological Analysis.* San Francisco: W. H. Freeman.

Kritzer, Herbert M. 1984. "Formal and Informal Theories of Negotiations: Paths to Understanding the Settlement Process in Ordinary Litigation." Paper presented at the annual meeting of the Law and Society Association, Boston. June 9, 1984.

———. 1991. *Let's Make a Deal.* Madison: University of Wisconsin Press.

Kritzer, Herbert M., Austin Sarat, David M. Trubek, and William L. F. Felstiner. 1985. "Winners and Losers in Litigation: Does Anyone Come Out Ahead?" Paper presented at the annual meeting of the Midwest Political Science Association, Chicago. April 19, 1985.

Kulat, Randy. 1984. "Hairy Tales from Chicago's Pro Se Court Where You Don't Need a Lawyer to Help Solve Some of Life's More Vexing Problems." *Student Lawyer* (September): 14-15.

Landes, William M., and Richard A. Posner. 1987. *The Economic Structure of Tort Law.* Cambridge, Mass.: Harvard University Press.

Lane, Robert E. 1988. "Procedural Goods in a Democracy: How One Is Treated versus What One Gets." *Social Justice Research* 2, no. 3: 177-92.

Lawrence, Susan E. 1991a. "Justice, Democracy, Litigation, and Political Participation." *Social Science Quarterly* 72: 464-77.

————. 1991b. "Participation through Mobilization of the Law: Institutions Providing Indigents with Access to the Civil Courts." *Polity* 23: 423–42.

Leventhal, Gerald S. 1980. "What Should Be Done with Equity Theory?" Pp. 27–55 in *Social Exchange: Advances in Theory and Research*, ed. K. J. Gergen, M. S. Greenberg, and R. H. Weiss. New York: Plenum Press.

Levi, Edward. 1949. *An Introduction to Legal Reasoning.* Chicago: University of Chicago Press.

Lewis, Anthony. 1964. *Gideon's Trumpet.* New York: Random House.

Lind, E. Allan. 1990. *Arbitrating High Stakes Cases: An Evaluation of Court-Annexed Arbitration in a United States District Court.* Santa Monica, Calif.: RAND Institute for Civil Justice.

————. 1991. "Perspective and Procedural Justice: Attorney and Litigant Evaluations of Court Procedures." *American Bar Foundation Working Paper Series,* no. 9106.

————. 1994. "Procedural Justice and Culture: Evidence for Ubiquitous Process Concerns." *Zeitschrift für Rechtssoziologie* 15: 24–36.

Lind, E. Allan, Yuen J. Huo, and Tom R. Tyler. 1994. ". . . And Justice for All: Ethnicity, Gender, and Preferences for Dispute Resolution Procedures." *Law and Human Behavior* 18: 269–90.

Lind, E. Allan, Ruth Kanfer, and P. Christopher Earley. 1990. "Voice, Control, and Procedural Justice: Instrumental and Noninstrumental Concerns in Fairness Judgements." *Journal of Personality and Social Psychology* 59: 952–59.

Lind, E. Allan, Robert J. MacCoun, Patricia A. Ebener, William L. F. Felstiner, Deborah R. Hensler, Judith Resnik, and Tom R. Tyler. 1989. *The Perception of Justice: Tort Litigants' Views of Trial, Court-Annexed Arbitration, and Judicial Settlement Conferences.* Santa Monica, Calif.: RAND Institute for Civil Justice.

————. 1990. *In the Eye of the Beholder: Tort Litigants' Evaluations of Their Experiences in the Civil Justice System.* Santa Monica, Calif.: RAND Institute for Civil Justice.

Lind, E. Allan, and Tom R. Tyler. 1988. *The Social Psychology of Procedural Justice.* New York: Plenum Press.

Lindblom, Charles E., and David Braybrooke. 1963. *A Strategy of Decision: Policy Evaluation as a Social Process.* New York: Free Press of Glencoe.

Littleton, Christine A. 1992. "Dispelling Myths about Sexual Harrassment: How the Senate Failed Twice." *Southern California Law Review* 65: 1419-29.

Loftus, Elizabeth F., and Willem A. Wagenaar. 1988. "Lawyers' Predictions of Success." *Jurimetrics Journal* 29: 437-53.

Long, Susan B., and Judyth A. Swingen. 1991. "Taxpayer Compliance: Setting New Agendas for Research." *Law and Society Review* 25: 637-83.

Lukacs, Georg. 1968. *History and Class Consciousness.* Trans. Rodney Livingstone. Cambridge, Mass.: MIT Press.

MacCoun, Robert J., E. Allan Lind, Deborah R. Hensler, David L. Bryant, and Patricia A. Ebener. 1988. *Alternative Adjudication: An Evaluation of the New Jersey Automobile Arbitration Program.* Santa Monica, Calif.: RAND Institute for Civil Justice.

MacCoun, Robert J., E. Allan Lind, and Tom R. Tyler. 1992. "Alternative Dispute Resolution in Trial and Appellate Courts." Pp. 95-118 in *Handbook of Psychology and Law*, ed. D. K. Kagehiro and W. S. Laufer. New York: Springer-Verlag.

Major, Brenda, Wayne H. Bylsma, and Catherine Cozzarelli. 1989. "Gender Differences in Distributive Justice Preferences: The Impact of Domain." *Sex Roles: A Journal of Research* 21, nos. 7-8: 487-97.

Malsch, Marijke. 1989. *Lawyers' Predictions of Judicial Decisions: A Study of Calibration of Experts.* Leiden, Netherlands: Rijksuniversiteit Leiden.

Marable, Manning. 1991. *Race: Reform or Rebellion.* Jackson: University Press of Mississippi.

Marx, Karl, and Friedrich Engels. 1965. *The German Ideology.* London: Lawrence and Wishart.

Mather, Lynn, and Barbara Yngvesson. 1980-81. "Language, Audience, and the Transformation of Disputes." *Law and Society Review* 15: 775-82.

McCann, Michael. 1992. "Reform Litigation on Trial." *Law and Social Inquiry* 17: 715-43.

———. 1994. *Rights at Work*. Chicago: University of Chicago Press.

———. 1996. "Causal versus Constitutive Explanations or, On the Difficulty of Being So Positive . . ." *Law and Social Inquiry* 21: 457–82.

McCloskey, Robert G. 1994. *The American Supreme Court*. Chicago: University of Chicago Press.

McCoin, Susan. 1993. "Dealing with Pro Se Litigants: Judges' Strategies in the Search for Legal Competence." Paper presented at the annual meeting of the Law and Society Association, Chicago, Illinois. May 28, 1993.

McEwen, Craig A., and Richard J. Maiman. 1984. "Mediation in Small Claims Court: Achieving Compliance through Consent." *Law and Society Review* 18: 11–49.

———. 1986. "The Relative Significance of Disputing Forum and Dispute Characteristics for Outcome and Compliance." *Law and Society Review* 20: 439–47.

McGraw, Kathleen M., and John T. Scholz. 1991. "Appeals to Civic Virtue versus Attention to Self-Interest: Effects on Tax Compliance." *Law and Society Review* 25: 471–98.

Meador, Daniel J. 1974. *Appellate Courts: Staff and Process in the Crisis of Volume*. St. Paul, Minn.: West Publishing.

Merry, Sally Engle. 1979. "Going to Court: Strategies of Dispute Management in an American Urban Neighborhood." *Law and Society Review* 13: 891–925.

———. 1990. *Getting Justice and Getting Even: Legal Consciousness among Working-Class Americans*. Chicago: University of Chicago Press.

Merry, Sally Engle, and Susan Silbey. 1984. "What Do Plaintiffs Want? Reexamining the Concept of Dispute." *Justice System Journal* 9: 151–78.

Mnookin, Robert H., and Lewis Kornhauser. 1979. "Bargaining in the Shadow of the Law." *Yale Law Journal* 88: 950–97.

Monsma, Karl, and Richard Lempert. 1992. "The Value of Counsel: 20 Years of Representation before a Public Housing Eviction Board." *Law and Society Review* 26: 627–67.

Moore, Barrington, Jr. 1978. *Injustice: The Social Bases of Obedience and Revolt*. New York. M. E. Sharpe.

Morrow, Phyllis. 1993. "When Compliance Isn't Consent: Discourse Conventions in a Cross-Cultural Courtroom." Unpublished paper, University of Alaska, Fairbanks.

Mueller, Michael. 1984. "Abusive Pro Se Plaintiffs in the Federal Courts: Proposals for Judicial Control." *Journal of Law Reform* 18: 93–165.

Muir, William K. 1967. *Law and Attitude Change*. Chicago: University of Chicago Press.

Musante, L., M. A. Gilbert, and John Thibaut. 1983. "The Effects of Control on the Perceived Fairness of Procedures and Outcomes." *Journal of Experimental Social Psychology* 19: 223–38.

New York State Bar Association Subcommittee on Pro Se Litigation. 1988. "Pro Se Litigation in the Second Circuit." *St. John's Law Review* 62: 571–83.

Nisbett, Richard E., and Timothy D. Wilson. 1977. "Telling More Than We Can Know: Verbal Reports on Mental Processes." *Psychological Review* 84: 231–59.

Nozick, Robert. 1974. *Anarchy, State, and Utopia*. New York: Basic Books.

O'Barr, William M., and John M. Conley. 1985. "Litigant Satisfaction versus Legal Adequacy in Small Claims Court Narratives." *Law and Society Review* 19: 661–701.

———. 1988. "Lay Expectations of the Civil Justice System." *Law and Society Review* 22: 137–61.

———. 1990. *Rules versus Relationships*. Chicago: University of Chicago Press.

Olson, Mancur. 1965. *The Logic of Collective Action*. Cambridge, Mass.: Harvard University Press.

Olson, Susan M. 1984. *Clients and Lawyers: Securing the Rights of Disabled Persons*. Westport, Conn.: Greenwood Press.

Paese, Paul W. 1986. *Procedural Fairness and Work Group Responses to Performance Evaluation Procedures*. Master's thesis, University of Illinois, Champaign.

Paese, Paul W., E. Allan Lind, and Ruth Kanfer. 1988. "Procedural Fairness and Work Group Responses to Performance Evaluation Systems." *Social Justice Research* 2, no. 3: 193–205.

Pitkin, Hanna F. 1967. *The Concept of Representation*. Berkeley: University of California Press.

Popovich, Peter S., Chief Judge. 1987. *Beginning a Judicial Tradition: Formative Years of the Minnesota Court of Appeals*. St. Paul, Minn.: State Court Administrator's Office.

Posner, Richard A. 1985. *The Federal Courts*. Cambridge, Mass.: Harvard University Press.

———. 1986. *Economic Analysis of Law*. 3d ed. Boston: Little, Brown.

———. 1996. *The Federal Courts: Challenge and Reform*. Cambridge, Mass.: Harvard University Press.

Poythress, Norman G. 1994. "Procedural Preferences, Perceptions of Fairness, and Compliance with Outcomes: A Study of Alternatives to the Standard Adversary Trial Procedure." *Law and Human Behavior*. 18: 361–76.

Rathjen, Gregory J. 1978. "Lawyers and the Appellate Choice: An Analysis of Factors Affecting the Decision to Appeal." *American Politics Quarterly* 6, no. 4: 387–405.

Rawls, John. 1971. *A Theory of Justice*. Cambridge, Mass.: Harvard University Press.

Raymond, Paul. 1992. "The Impact of a Televised Trial on Individuals' Information and Attitudes." *Judicature* 75, no. 4: 204–9.

Richardson, Laurel. 1990. *Writing Strategies: Reaching Diverse Audiences*. Qualitative Research Methods, vol. 21. Newbury Park, Calif.: Sage.

Robbins, Ira P., and Susan N. Herman. 1976. "Litigating without Counsel: *Faretta* or for Worse." *Brooklyn Law Review* 42: 629–84.

Rosenberg, Gerald. 1991. *The Hollow Hope*. Chicago: University of Chicago Press.

———. 1996. "Positivism, Interpretivism, and the Study of Law." *Law and Social Inquiry* 21: 435–56.

Rosenberg, Maurice. 1965. "Court Congestion: Status, Causes, and Proposed Remedies." Pp. 29–59 in *The Courts, the Public, and the Law Explosion*, ed. Harry W. Jones. Englewood Cliffs, N.J.: Prentice-Hall.

Rosenthal, Douglas E. 1974. *Lawyer and Client: Who's in Charge?* New York: Russell Sage.

Rutherford, Jane. 1992. "The Myth of Due Process." *Boston University Law Review* 72: 1–99.

Sarat, Austin, and William L. F. Felstiner. 1986. "Law and Strategy in the Divorce Lawyer's Office." *Law and Society Review* 20: 93–134.

———. 1988. "Law and Social Relations: Vocabularies of Motive in Lawyer/ Client Interaction." *Law and Society Review* 22: 737–69.

———. 1989. "Lawyers and Legal Consciousness: Law Talk in the Divorce Lawyer's Office." *Yale Law Journal* 98: 1663–88.

———. 1995. *Divorce Lawyers and Their Clients.* New York: Oxford University Press.

Sarat, Austin, and Joel B. Grossman. 1975. "Courts and Conflict Resolution: Problems in the Mobilization of Adjudication." *American Political Science Review* 69: 1200–17.

Scarbrough, Elinor. 1984. *Political Ideology and Voting.* Oxford: Clarendon Press.

Scheingold, Stuart A. 1974. *The Politics of Rights.* New Haven, Conn.: Yale University Press.

Schroeder, Christine. 1992. "Congress Stories." *Southern California Law Review* 65: 1530–67.

Schubert, Glendon. 1965. *Judicial Policy-Making.* Chicago: Scott, Foresman.

Schuck, Peter H. 1986. "The Role of Judges in Settling Complex Cases: The Agent Orange Example." *University of Chicago Law Review* 53: 337–65.

Scott, James C. 1985. *Weapons of the Weak.* New Haven, Conn.: Yale University Press.

———. 1990. *Domination and the Art of Resistance: Hidden Transcripts.* New Haven, Conn.: Yale University Press.

Segal, Jeffrey, and Albert Cover. 1989. "Ideological Values and the Votes of U.S. Supreme Court Justices." *American Political Science Review* 83: 557–64.

Shamir, Ronen. 1990. "Landmark Cases and the Reproduction of Legitimacy: The Case of Israel's High Court of Justice." *Law and Society Review* 24: 781–805.

———. 1991. "Litigation as a Consummatory Action: The Instrumental Paradigm Reconsidered." *Studies in Law, Politics, and Society* 11: 41–68.

Shapiro, Martin. 1980. "Appeal." *Law and Society Review* 14: 629–61.

Simon, Jonathan. 1992. "Review Essay: 'The Long Walk Home' to Politics." *Law and Society Review* 26: 923–41.

Skogan, Wesley G. 1989. "The Social Stratification of Procedural Justice." Unpublished paper, Northwestern University.

Slider, Patti. 1992. "Court House Violence—It Happens in Kansas." *Journal of the Kansas Bar Association* 61: 17.

Solimine, Michael E. 1990. "Revitalizing Interlocutory Appeals in the Federal Courts." *George Washington Law Review* 58: 1165–213.

Songer, Donald R., Charles M. Cameron, and Jeffrey A. Segal. 1995. "An Empirical Test of the Rational-Actor Theory of Litigation." *Journal of Politics* 57: 1119–29.

Songer, Donald R., and Reginald Sheehan. 1989. "Supreme Court Impact on Compliance and Outcomes." *Western Political Quarterly* 45: 297–316.

———. 1992. "Who Wins on Appeal: Upperdogs and Underdogs in the United States Courts of Appeals." *American Journal of Political Science* 36: 235–58.

Stalans, Loretta J. 1991. "Citizens' Procedural Expectations for an Upcoming Tax Audit: Their Nature and Formation." *American Bar Foundation Working Paper Series,* no. 9107.

———. 1994. "Forming Procedural Expectations about Unfamiliar Legal Arenas: Do People Generalize from Loosely Related Past Legal Experiences?" *Psychology, Crime and Law* 1: 39–57.

Stalans, Loretta J., and Karyl A. Kinsey. 1994. "Self-Presentation and Legal Socialization in Society: Available Messages about Personal Tax Audits." *Law and Society Review* 28: 859–96.

Stevens, John W. 1988. "Violence in the Halls of Justice." *North Carolina State Bar Quarterly.* 88: 20.

Thibaut, John, and Laurens Walker. 1975. *Procedural Justice: A Psychological Analysis.* New York: John Wiley.

Tushnet, Mark V. 1987. *The NAACP's Legal Strategy against Segregated Education, 1925–1950.* Chapel Hill: University of North Carolina Press.

Tyler, Tom R. 1994. "Governing amid Diversity: The Effect of Fair Decisionmaking Procedures on the Legitimacy of Government." *Law and Society Review* 28: 809–31.

———. 1984. "The Role of Perceived Injustice in Defendants' Evaluations of Their Courtroom Experience." *Law and Society Review* 18: 51–75.

———. 1988a. "What Is Procedural Justice?: Criteria Used by Citizens to Assess the Fairness of Legal Procedures." *Law and Society Review* 22: 103–35.

———. 1988b. "Procedural Justice Research." *Social Justice Research* 1: 41–65.

———. 1990. *Why People Obey the Law.* New Haven, Conn.: Yale University Press.

Tyler, Tom R., Jonathan D. Casper, and Bonnie Fisher. 1989. "Maintaining Allegiance toward Political Authorities: The Role of Prior Attitudes and the Use of Fair Procedures." *American Journal of Political Science* 33: 629–52.

Tyler, Tom R., and Gregory Mitchell. 1994. "Legitimacy and the Empowerment of Discretionary Legal Authority: The United States Supreme Court and Abortion Rights." *Duke Law Journal* 43: 703–815.

Tyler, Tom R., and Ken Rasinski. 1991. "Procedural Justice, Institutional Legitimacy, and the Acceptance of Unpopular U.S. Supreme Court Decisions: A Reply to Gibson." *Law and Society Review* 25: 621–30.

Van Koppen, Peter J., and Marijke Malsch. 1991. "Defendants and One-Shotters Win after All: Compliance with Court Decisions in Civil Cases." *Law and Society Review* 25: 803–20.

Wasby, Stephen. 1970. *The Impact of the United States Supreme Court: Some Perspectives.* Homewood, Ill.: Dorsey Press.

———. 1995. *Race Relations Litigation in an Age of Complexity.* Charlottesville: University of Virginia Press.

Wax, Jack. 1992. "Stop Violence in the Courthouse." *National Law Journal* 14 (August 24): p. 17.

Webster's New Twentieth Century Dictionary. 1970. Springfield, Mass.: Merriam-Webster.

Weiss, Nancy. 1983. *Farewell to the Party of Lincoln: Black Politics in the Age of FDR.* Princeton, N.J.: Princeton University Press.

Wemmers, Jo-Anne. 1995. "Victims in the Dutch Criminal Justice System: The Effects of Treatment on Victims' Attitudes and Compliance." *International Review of Victimology* 3: 323-41.

Weschler, Herbert. 1959. "Toward Neutral Principles of Constitutional Law." *Harvard Law Review* 73: 1-35.

Wheeler, Stanton, Bliss Cartwright, Robert A. Kagan, and Lawrence M. Friedman. 1987. "Do the 'Haves' Come Out Ahead? Winning and Losing in State Supreme Courts, 1870-1970." *Law and Society Review* 21: 403-45.

Wissler, Roselle L. 1995. "Mediation and Adjudication in Small Claims Court: The Effects of Process and Case Characteristics." *Law and Society Review* 29: 323-58.

Wittman, Donald. 1988. "Dispute Resolution, Bargaining, and the Selection of Cases for Trial: A Study of Biased and Unbiased Data." *Journal of Legal Studies* 17: 313-52.

Wood, Allen W. 1980. "The Marxian Critique of Justice." Pp. 3-41 in *Marx, Justice, and History,* ed. Marshall Cohen, Thomas Nagel, and Thomas Scanlan. Princeton, N.J.: Princeton University Press.

Wright, Brian H. 1993. "The Formal Inquiry Approach: Balancing a Defendant's Right to Proceed Pro Se with a Defendant's Right to Assistance of Counsel." *Marquette Law Review* 76: 785-804.

Wright, Ronald G. 1984. "Constitutional Law: The Sixth Amendment Right of Self-Representation and the Role of Standby Counsel." *Washburn Law Journal* 24: 164-74.

Yankelovich, Skelly, and White, Inc. 1977. *The Public Image of Courts: Highlights of a National Survey of the General Public, Judges, Lawyers and Community Leaders.* Report prepared for the National Center for State Courts. Washington, D.C.

Young, Rowland L. 1984. "Pro Se Defendant's Rights Not Infringed by Standby Counsel." *ABA Journal* 70: 112.

Zeigler, Donald H., and Michele G. Hermann. 1972. "The Invisible Litigant: An Inside View of Pro Se Actions in the Federal Courts." *New York University Law Review* 47: 157–257.

Zemans, Frances Zahn. 1983. "Legal Mobilization: The Neglected Role of the Law in the Political System." *American Political Science Review* 77: 690–702.

Index